Mr. Gorbachev, Tear Down This Wall

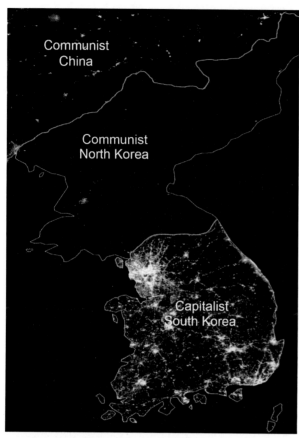

Let Them Come to Pyongyang: A Satellite Photo of North and South Korea at Night

Well over half a century ago, in his famous "Ich bin ein Berliner" speech (June 26, 1963), President John F. Kennedy aptly compared communal Socialism to free market Democracy with the following:

"There are many people in the world who really don't understand, or say they don't, what is the great issue between the free world and the Communist world. Let them come to Berlin. There are some who say that communism is the wave of the future. Let them come to Berlin. And there are some who say in Europe and elsewhere we can work with the Communists. Let them come to Berlin. And there are even a few who say that it is true that communism is an evil system, but it permits us to make economic progress. Lass' sie nach Berlin kommen. Let them come to Berlin."

Fast forward 53 years later to a satellite photo of North Korea and South Korea. The picture to the left is a direct pictorial quote of President Kennedy's speech.

The photo, taken at night, shows an almost completely dark North Korea and China with small light clusters, both of which stand in deep contrast to the brightness of South Korea. The difference in energy distribution highlights the immense economic disparity witnessed in the region.

President Kennedy's timeless message is as true today as it was then—Let them come to Pyongyang.

A Template for Understanding the Economy

By two good friends who share a common view of the world in which we live.

Arthur B. Laffer, Ph.D.

&

Rex Sinquefield

Arthur B. Laffer, Ph.D. is the founder and chairman of Laffer Associates, an economic research and consulting firm. Dr. Laffer is best known for the Laffer Curve, a diagrammatic representation of the relationship between tax rates and tax revenues. His work has been credited with triggering a worldwide tax-cutting movement in the 1980s, earning him the distinction in many publications as "The Father of Supply-Side Economics." One of his earliest successes in shaping public policy was his involvement in Proposition 13, the groundbreaking California initiative that drastically cut property taxes in the state in 1978. A member of President Reagan's Economic Policy Advisory Board for both of Reagan's terms, Dr. Laffer also served as the first Chief Economist of the OMB under George Shultz and advised Prime Minister Margaret Thatcher on fiscal policy in the U.K. during the 1980s. He has been a faculty member at the University of Chicago, University of Southern California and Pepperdine University. Dr. Laffer received a B.A. in economics from Yale University and received an MBA and a Ph.D. in economics from Stanford University.

Rex Sinquefield, often referred to as one of the world's leading financial gurus, now spends most of his time and resources dedicated to philanthropic causes and improving his home state's tax and education policy. Raised in Saint Vincent Orphanage in Saint Louis, Sinquefield earned a business degree from Saint Louis University and an MBA from the University of Chicago, where he studied under Eugene Fama, the father of efficient markets. He went on to develop some of the nation's first index funds, and, along with associate David Booth, formed Dimensional Fund Advisors in 1981, which today oversees more than $500 billion in global assets (April 2017). After retiring in 2005, Sinquefield returned to his much loved State of Missouri, where he co-founded and serves as president of the Show-Me Institute, the state's only free-market think tank. Rex and his wife Dr. Jeanne Sinquefield have become some of Missouri's most important philanthropists. Philanthropic priorities include the Chess Club and Scholastic Center of Saint Louis, Saint Louis the World Chess Hall of Fame and the Mizzou New Music Initiative at the University of Missouri-Columbia.

Acknowledgments

Bob Bartley, Jude Wanniski and Bob Mundell were our three steadfast partners at the creation. And to them we dedicate this Template for Understanding the Economy with our deepest gratitude.

This Template for Understanding the Economy is a collection of self-contained chronicles illustrating the powerful role of incentives in affecting the outcomes of economic policies. The object lessons from these stories are as clear as instructions can be. Throughout this Template for Understanding the Economy, statements by a great many observers, who know or should know, have been sprinkled liberally.

This template would never have seen the light of day were it not for the selfless efforts of Tony Batman, David Booth, Joel Citron, Jim Dondero, Bill Fickling Jr. and his son Roy Fickling. The partnership and co-authorship between Arthur Laffer and Rex Sinquefield is ideal for this Template.

Five people deserve special thanks for reviewing earlier drafts of the Template and providing helpful and detailed comments. A big tip of the hat goes to David Kretschmer, Ryan George, Rowena Itchon, Brian Domitrovic, and the love of Arthur Laffer's life, Traci Laffer.

In addition, we are grateful to Matson Money, 1st Global and the team at Laffer Associates, whose efforts were indispensable—Julia Roseman, Kristen Moser, Nick Drinkwater and John Burke.

We have also borrowed freely from all sorts of people, including, of course, two current colleagues in arms, Larry Kudlow and Stephen Moore, as well as Jerry Brown, Steven Heinz, John Childs, Rizwan Rawji, Bob Murphy, the late Jude Wanniski, Don Rumsfeld, Casey Mulligan, Larry Gatlin, the late Milton Friedman, Travis and Kelly Brown, George Shultz, Robert Mundell, Dan Mitchell, the late Jack Kemp, Bruce Bartlett, Richard Vedder, Bill Shiebler, Beau Duncan and many others.

Contents

Section I – Heroes, Villains, Triumphs, Failures, and Other Memorable Events

Government should not be in the business of picking winners and losers and using taxpayer dollars to back their bets. If markets work, then markets work. It is just that simple. If seasoned investors can't outguess markets, then government officials should not try to do so either.
— Rex Sinquefield, Forbes, 2013[1]

And just for the record, the ideal code of conduct is wonderfully expressed by President Theodore Roosevelt in 1905:

Take what the toastmaster was kind enough to say as to my standing for a square deal. I want that understood literally. I do not want it exaggerated on one side or the other. When I say I believe in a square deal I do not mean, and nobody who speaks the truth can mean, that he believes it possible to give every man the best hand. If the cards do not come to any man, or if they do come, and he has not got the power to play them, that is his affair. All I mean is that there shall not be any crookedness in the dealing...

All any of us can pretend to do is to come as near as our imperfect abilities will allow to securing through governmental agencies an equal opportunity for each man to show the stuff that is in him; and that must be done with no more intention of discrimination against the rich man than the poor man, or against the poor man than the rich man; with the intention of safeguarding each man, rich or poor, poor or rich, in his rights, and giving him as nearly as may be a fair chance to do what his powers permit him to do; always provided he does not wrong his neighbor.
— Theodore Roosevelt, 1905[2]

---

[1] Rex Sinquefield, "Eugene Fama's Efficient Market Is A Sound Guiding Principle For Investors And Policymakers," Forbes, Oct 17, 2013.
[2] Theodore Roosevelt, Works, p. 322, June 6, 1905.

Hedgehog Versus the Fox – The Fox knows many things while the Hedgehog knows only one thing, but it is one big thing —Hauser's Law

In the 1990s San Francisco money manager Kurt Hauser published a paper outlining "Hauser's law" to wit: No matter what tax rates were, Federal Tax Revenues as a share of GDP didn't change. Just look:

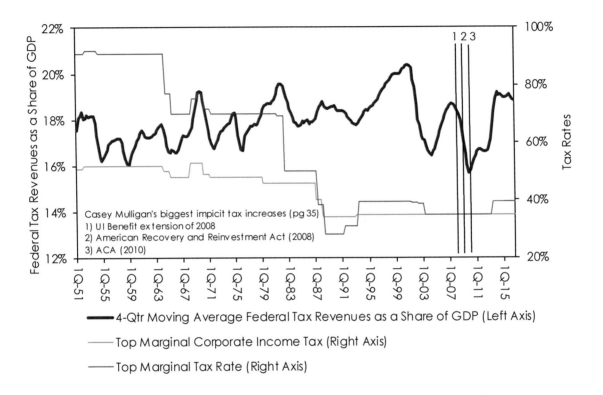

If tax revenues as a share of GDP are, in fact, constant (or at the very least trendless) then any reasonable[3] increases in tax rates will be more than offset by decreases in actual tax bases so that diminished tax revenues decline proportionally with diminished GDP. Symmetrically, any reasonable decreases in tax rates will also be more than offset by increases in actual tax bases so that expanded tax revenues increase proportionally with increased GDP. This law of Hauser's is a very big idea! In 1993 he wrote:

> *The historical record is quite simple, if surprising. No matter what the tax rates have been, in postwar America tax revenues have remained at about 19.5% of GDP... If history is any guide, higher taxes will not increase the government's take as a percentage of the economy.*

---

[3] Reasonable here means within the ranges of past actual experience

Over the past 44 years (remember he was only using data up to and including 1992) *there have been 25 substantive changes in the federal tax codes, with the top marginal personal income tax rate ranging as high as 92% and as low as 28%. The period has also witnessed numerous changes in corporate tax rates, investment tax credits, surtaxes, excise taxes, capital gains taxes, and depreciation schedules.*

…a review of the major tax bills—such as the Revenue Act of 1964, the Revenue and Expenditure Control Act of 1968, the Economic Recovery Act of 1981, the Tax Reform Act of 1986, and the Omnibus Budget Reconciliation Act of 1990, among others—indicates that revenues as a percentage of GDP in the two years prior to changes in tax rates were not meaningfully different from those in the two years following. There is no correlation between tax rate changes and government revenues as a share of GDP.

…Thanks to Arthur Laffer, we know that a tax of 100% will not collect 100% of the income.

Raising taxes encourages taxpayers to shift, hide and underreport income. The creative rich will avoid paying higher taxes while the less creative rich will pay more taxes, one offsetting the other.

There is no economic theory, be it classical, neoclassical, Keynesian, supply-side or Marxist, that promotes higher taxes as a stimulus to economic activity… Thus under a tax increase, the numerator, revenues, will rise less than the forecast, while GDP, the denominator, will also advance less than the forecast—but the quotient, percentage collected, will be the same.

…Thus under a tax reduction, revenues will rise to a greater degree than would otherwise be the case; GDP will also advance more than forecast, but, again, the quotient, percentage collected, will adjust to the 19.5% mean.

…In the postwar period, economic activity, as measured by GDP, has accelerated in the four quarters following a lowering of tax rates, while GDP has experienced a decline in growth rates in the four quarters following tax hikes.

Mirror, Mirror on the Wall, Who is the Fairest of Them All?
Obama vs. Reagan, Kennedy and Trump

It should be known that at the beginning of the dynasty, taxation yields a large revenue from small assessments. At the end of the dynasty, taxation yields a small revenue from large assessments.[4]
— Ibn Khaldun, The Muqaddimah, 1381

Tax Rate Increases Under Obama in 2015

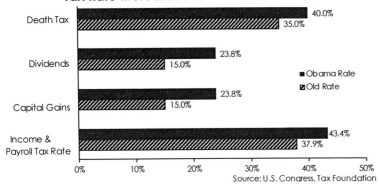

Source: U.S. Congress, Tax Foundation

Taxes ↑ ☹

Taxation, pushed to the extreme, has the lamentable effect of impoverishing the individual, without enriching the state.
— Jean-Baptiste Say,
A Treatise on Political Economy, 1851

Tax Rate Decreases Under Reagan – Two Terms

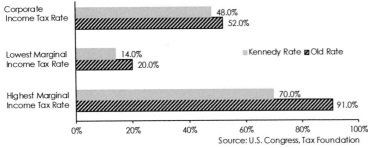

Source: U.S. Congress, Tax Foundation

Despite the 'assurances,' 'promises,' 'pledges' and 'commitments' you are given, the spending cuts have a way of being forgotten or quietly lobbied out of future budgets. But the tax increases are as certain to come as death and taxes.
—President Ronald Reagan, 1993

Tax Rate Decreases Under Kennedy in 1964*

Source: U.S. Congress, Tax Foundation

*Under President Kennedy's watch there was also a 7% investment tax credit, accelerated depreciation schedule, and the Kennedy Round 35% reduction in taxes on traded products

Taxes ↓ ☺

Tax Rate Decreases Under Trump – First Year*

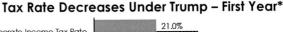
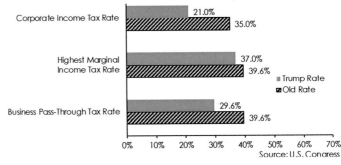

Source: U.S. Congress

*The Trump tax law repeals the Obamacare individual mandate, shifts corporate taxation from a global system to a territorial system, and allows all capital expenditures to be expensed for the five years 2018-2022.

---

[4] Ibn Khaldun, The Muqaddimah (Franz Rosenthal trans.), p. 230, 1967.

We are the Champions — Queen
Measuring the Presidents' Economic Performance

Real GDP Per Adult Detrended
(quarterly, 1Q-50 to 3Q-16)

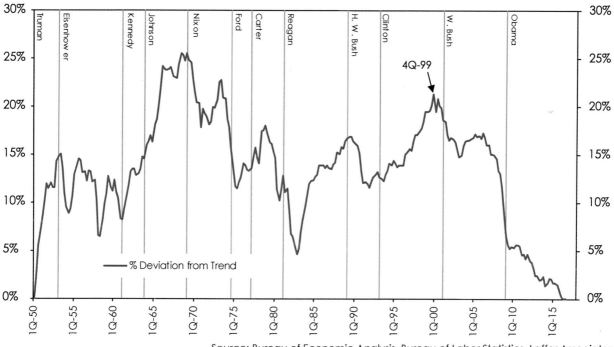

Source: Bureau of Economic Analysis, Bureau of Labor Statistics, Laffer Associates

The proper measure of the performance of the U.S. economy is detrended real Gross Domestic Product (GDP) per adult. GDP is a direct measure of all of the goods and services produced in the U.S. Adjusting GDP for price level changes yields real GDP. We adjust real GDP for the number of adults to facilitate cross-section comparisons. We detrend real GDP per adult (in the chart above from first quarter 1950 through the third quarter of 2016) to allow comparisons over time. Thus, every point on the above chart shows the percentage above trend or below trend of real GDP per adult. Increases or decreases in real GDP per adult detrended represents growth in excess of trend or below trend.

This chart shows the enormous growth under President Kennedy, the levelling off under President Johnson and the veritable collapse under Presidents Nixon, Ford and Carter. And there is the long period of expansion under Presidents Reagan and Clinton, with the mild setback under President George H.W. Bush. But, the real tragedy begins in 2001 with Presidents George W. Bush and Barack Obama. Not surprisingly, for the whole period 1950-2016, the U.S. is at its lowest level in 66 years in 2016. And yet read what they said:

At this moment—with a growing economy, shrinking deficits, bustling industry, and booming energy production—we have risen from recession freer to write our own future than any other nation on Earth.[5]
— President Barack Obama, 2015 State of the Union

 This theory that Governor Reagan is talking about is what I call a 'voodoo economic' policy.[6]
— George H.W. Bush, 1980

 My opponent won't rule out raising taxes. But I will. And the Congress will push me to raise taxes and I'll say no. And they'll push, and I'll say no, and they'll push again, and I'll say, to them, 'Read my lips: no new taxes.'[7]
— George H.W. Bush, 1988 Republican National Convention

 I see a future of economic security—security that will come from tapping our own great resources of oil and gas, coal and sunlight, and from building the tools and technology and factories for a revitalized economy based on jobs and stable prices for everyone.[8]
— Jimmy Carter, 1980, Democratic Nomination Acceptance Speech

[5] "Remarks by the President in State of Union Address," The White House, January 20, 2015.
[6] Margaret Miner and Hugh Rawson, The Oxford Dictionary of American Quotations, p. 210, 2006. https://books.google.com/books?id=whg05Z4Nwo0C&printsec=frontcover#v=onepage&q&f=false
[7] "1988 George H.W. Bush Speech," August 18, 1988. https://www.c-span.org/video/?c4537578/read-lips-new-taxes
[8] Jimmy Carter, "Remarks Accepting the Presidential Nomination at the 1980 Democratic National Convention in New York," August 14, 1980. http://www.presidency.ucsb.edu/ws/?pid=44909

Reaganomics vs. Obamanomics: $3.5 Trillion Growth Gap

We probably managed this [the U.S. economy] better than any large economy on Earth in modern history.
— President Barack Obama, New York Times, 2016

In short, this tax program will increase our wealth far more than it increases our public debt. The actual burden of that debt--as measured in relation to our total output--will decline. To continue to increase our debt as the result of inadequate earnings is a sign of weakness. But to borrow prudently in order to invest in a tax revision that will greatly increase our earning power can be a source of strength.
—John F. Kennedy, Tax Message to Congress, 1963

It is a central axiom of the supply-side people that it is easier to get people to produce more than it is to persuade them to do with less.
—William F. Buckley

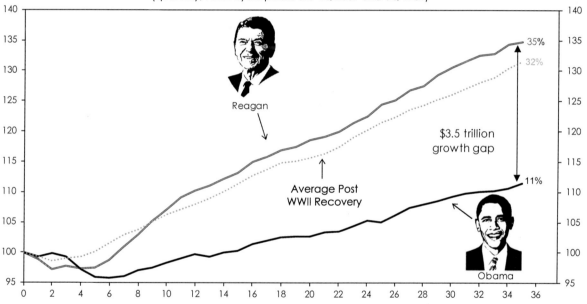

Real GDP: Recoveries Indexed to NBER Cycle Peak = 100
(quarterly, NBER cycle peaks are 4Q-2007 and 3Q-1981)

Source: Bureau of Economic Analysis, National Bureau of Economic Research, Laffer Associates

The strength of any economic recovery is the rate of GDP growth in real terms, and the Obama recovery ranks as the single worst recovery in recent U.S. history. If real GDP under President Obama had grown at the same rate as real GDP grew under President Reagan, 2016 real GDP would be $3.5 trillion higher—that's enough to cover the annual salary expense for 61,929,365 additional American workers at the U.S. real median household income of $56,516.

The Republican alternative is the biggest tax giveaway in history. They call it Reagan-Kemp-Roth; I call it a free lunch that Americans cannot afford. The Republican tax program offers rebates to the rich, deprivation for the poor, and fierce inflation for all of us. Their party's own Vice Presidential nominee said that Reagan-Kemp-Roth would result in an inflation rate of more than 30 percent. He called it "voodoo economics."
— President Jimmy Carter, Democratic Nomination Acceptance Speech, 1980

Consistently Great vs. Consistently Sub-Par

As Senator Barry Goldwater (R-AZ) said when he accepted the nomination for president at the 1964 Republican National Convention, *"Extremism in the defense of liberty is no vice. Moderation in pursuit of justice is no virtue."*

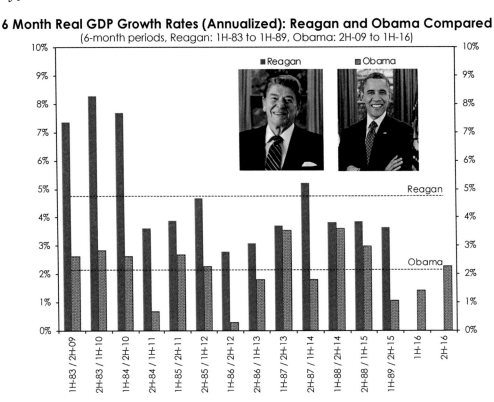

6 Month Real GDP Growth Rates (Annualized): Reagan and Obama Compared
(6-month periods, Reagan: 1H-83 to 1H-89, Obama: 2H-09 to 1H-16)

Source: Bureau of Economic Analysis

This chart shows the growth rate in real GDP each six-month period during the Reagan and Obama recoveries. In each and every six-month period from the start date of their respective economic recoveries, the growth rate in real GDP under President Reagan was higher than the corresponding growth rate in real GDP under President Obama. In fact, there wasn't one single six-month period under President Obama where economic growth annualized exceeded 3.6%, while 10 of the 13 six-month periods under President Reagan exceeded 3.6%. And just for the record, three six-month periods under President Reagan had annualized growth over 7%. Perhaps President Obama should have heeded his own words:

> *I think Ronald Reagan changed the trajectory of America in a way that Richard Nixon did not and in a way that Bill Clinton did not. He put us on a fundamentally different path because the country was ready for it...I think it's fair to say that the Republicans were the party of ideas for a pretty long chunk of time there over the last 10, 15 years, in the sense that they were challenging conventional wisdom.*[9]
> — Then-Senator Barack Obama, 2008

[9] "In his own words: Barack Obama on Ronald Reagan," February 4, 2008. http://latimesblogs.latimes.com/washington/2008/02/in-his-own-word.html

Search for the Missing Jobs

If government taxes people who work and pays people who don't work, don't be surprised if there are less people who work.
— *Jack Kemp, 1981*

Employment to Population: Reagan and Obama Compared
(months past NBER recession trough, Reagan: Nov-82 to Feb-90; Obama: Jun-09 to Sep-16)
Months Past NBER Recession Trough

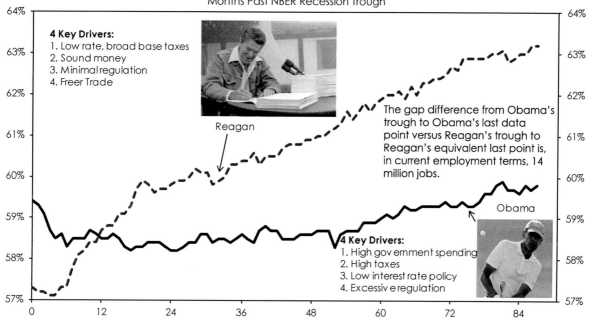

If President Obama's employment to adult population had risen by as much as President Reagan's employment to adult population, the U.S. would have had almost 14 million more jobs per year in 2016. Even more to the point, if 2016's employment to adult population were the equivalent of the employment to adult population peak witnessed in early 2000 under President Bill Clinton, we would have had around 12.7 million more jobs.

Will we accept an economy where only a few of us do spectacularly well? Or will we commit ourselves to an economy that generates rising incomes and chances for everyone who makes the effort?[10]
— *President Barack Obama, 2015 State of the Union*

Taxes should be cut and government spending maintained through deficit financing only when a special condition exists, a condition Mundell and Laffer say exists now. "There are always two tax rates that produce the same dollar revenues," says Laffer. "For example, when taxes are zero, revenues are zero. When taxes are 100 percent, there is no production, and revenues are also zero. In between these extremes there is one rate that maximizes government revenues." Any higher tax rate reduces total output and the tax base, and becomes counterproductive even for producing revenues. U.S. marginal tax rates are now, they argue, in this unproductive range and the economy is being "choked, asphyxiated by taxes," says Mundell. Tax rates have been put up inadvertently by the impact of inflation on all the progressivity of the tax structure.[11]
— *Jude Wanniski, The Public Interest, 1975*

---

[10] "Remarks by the President in State of Union Address," The White House, January 20, 2015.
https://www.whitehouse.gov/the-press-office/2015/01/20/remarks-president-state-union-address-january-20-2015
[11] Bruce Bartlett, "Supply-Side Economics: 'Voodoo Economics' or Lasting Contribution?" Laffer Associates, November 11, 2003.

Seven Keys to a Good Tax Policy[12] —Rizwan Rawji

Taxes that should be avoided are income tax (especially progressive) and small taxes where the costs of collection approach or exceed the revenue actually collected. The keys to good tax policy are:

i.) Tax these items most that can escape the least, and conversely tax those least that can easily escape. It makes no sense to tax something that then flees the jurisdiction, goes underground or stops working. You not only don't get the revenue, but you also lose the benefits of the productive services.

ii.) Tax those things most that you least like (sin taxes). An additional benefit or sin taxes is that they do reduce the activity being taxed.

iii.) Tax those things least where the collection costs are highest.

iv.) Broad-based low rate taxes provide people with the least incentives to evade, avoid and otherwise not report taxable income and the least number of places where they can escape taxation.

v.) Tax people fairly. People in like circumstances should have similar tax burdens. The perception of fairness is key to voluntary compliance.

vi.) Make sure that taxation is not arbitrary or easily subject to discretionary charges. The power to tax in the wrong hand is an ugly weapon for exploitation.

vii.) Lastly, collect only as much as you really need. Wasteful spending will always rise to the level of revenues.

These rules should help your efforts, if meticulously adhered to. Next to a bad money, I know of nothing that will bring an economy to its knees faster than an unjust, inefficient, anti-growth, excessive system of taxation. This principal is universal.

And in case you were in the mood for an eighth key, we could always turn to comedian Jackie Mason,

If we want [politicians] to be successful, put them on commission and don't pay them until they show a profit.
—Jackie Mason

---

[12] We are grateful to Rizwan Rawji who carries copies of the "seven keys" with him "at all times" and claims these keys were adopted from Professor Laffer's lectures.

Section II – Government Policy Actions: Income Redistribution

A government big enough to give you everything you want is big enough to take away everything you've got.[13]
— Ronald Reagan, 1984

Government redistributes income by taking income (the tax) from someone who earns more and giving the proceeds as a subsidy to someone who earns less. By taxing income from the person who earns more, that person's incentive to produce income declines, and he or she will produce/earn less.

Also, by giving the proceeds from the tax to someone who earns less (the subsidy), that person will now have an alternative source of income other than working and, therefore, will work less. Any government attempt to redistribute income will reduce total income, and the larger the redistribution, the larger the decline.

The reasoning behind this lies in what economists call the Slutsky equation, which breaks down the effects of a price change, tax rate change, or transfer into two components: an income effect and a substitution effect.[14] The substitution effect describes the change in consumption patterns that arise from a change in the relative price of goods—when the price of a good increases, consumers will choose to substitute less costly alternatives for these more expensive goods. In technical terms, the substitution effects of a redistributive tax/subsidy always work in the

---

[13] Ronald Reagan, "Remarks at a Reagan-Bush Rally in Warren, Michigan," October 10, 1984. http://www.presidency.ucsb.edu/ws/?pid=39215
[14] "Slutsky Equation," Wikipedia. https://en.wikipedia.org/wiki/Slutsky_equation The Slutsky equation also includes the "income" effects of a tax and subsidy as described above. The "income" effects for the whole economy, as opposed to the "substitution" effects, always cancel each other. The "income" effect for the taxpayer would be positive while the "income" effect for the subsidy recipient is negative.

same direction for both taxpayers and subsidy recipients, i.e. any and all redistributions reduce everyone's incentive to work and thus reduce total income.

The income effect describes the change in demand of a good as a result of a change in income or, alternatively, it is the amount of work hours/pre-tax income a consumer chooses to forego given a tax change. In an aggregate economy considering all participants, all income effects of a price change or a tax rate change or a transfer payment change will offset each other 100% as long as the proceeds of the taxes are distributed back to the people. In other words, the negative income effect of the taxpayer is offset by the positive income effect of the transfer recipient.

This reasoning can be seen in examples where we have higher tax rates and more generous transfers, in which the substitution effects incentivize both net tax payers and net transfer recipients to work less and demand more leisure. Here, again, the substitution effects are all that remain from a tax rate increase / transfer increase, which unambiguously leads to lower work, output and employment.

This is math, not politics or opinion. As long as people respond to incentives, all acts to redistribute income will be accompanied by a reduction in total income. And the more income is redistributed, the greater will be the reduction in total income.

In the extreme, imagine the example of a complete income redistribution where everyone who earns more than the average income is taxed 100% of the excess above the average, and everyone who earns less than the average income is subsidized 100% up to the average. Everyone will have the same after-tax, after-subsidy income regardless of their pre-tax, pre-subsidy income. If everyone who worked, no matter how hard, was only able to receive the average income and everyone who didn't work or worked very little also received the average income, in short order, all income will fall to zero. 100% redistribution equates to zero income/output.

It is not much of an exaggeration to say that all of economics results from inequality. Without inequality of priorities and capabilities, there would be no trade, no specialization, and no surpluses produced by cooperation.[15]
— Finis Welch, 1999

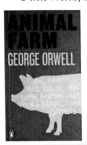

Somehow it seemed as though the farm had grown richer without making the animals themselves any richer—except, of course, for the pigs and the dogs.
— Chapter 10, Animal Farm, published in 1945

[15] Bruce Bartlett, "Wealth, Mobility, Inheritance and the Estate Tax," Laffer Associates, June 6, 2000.

Experienced Workforce on the Sidelines

I want to see the politics, the corruption, the campaign money taken out of that whole tax writing business and have one simple 13% tax, deduction for rent, home mortgage interest and charity and that's it. And then business 13%, and you can expense all equipment purchases the first year, and if you're on social security, you can earn whatever you want without losing your benefits.[16]
— *Gov. Jerry Brown, 1992*

Work Hours Per Adult
(annual, household survey data, 2007 to 2013)

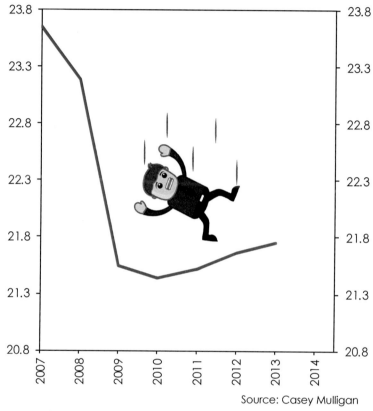

Source: Casey Mulligan

There are several reasons why the labor market remains continuously depressed— namely, the onset of major subsidies and regulations intended to help the poor and unemployed, yet that also severely reduce incentives to work and earn. As Casey Mulligan put it, "redistribution is a subsidy to layoffs."[17] People today are rewarded for looking, not for working, and employers today are less penalized for laying off workers. One major change lies in the Affordable Care Act, in which the government decided to claim responsibility and pay for health care if an individual was laid-off, whereas previously employers were required to pay for former-employee health insurance.

Casey Mulligan demonstrates this clearly in the above graph, in which data from the Bureau of Labor Statistics' household employment survey is plotted briefly before the Great Recession through 2013. The household survey asks respondents about their work status (and the status of other adults in the household) during a specific reference week. If the respondent was at work during that week, the survey asks for the number of hours worked. These hours worked, counting zeros for persons not at work (which includes those that want to work but cannot), can be averaged across respondents to arrive at another measure of hours worked per adult.[18]

Anthony Hopkins as his character Charles Morse in *The Edge*:
"We're all put to the test, but it never comes in the form or at the point we would prefer, does it?"

[16] Gov. Jerry Brown, 1992 Presidential Election, Democratic Candidates Debate, February 23, 1992.
[17]Casey B. Mulligan, "A Recovery Stymied by Redistribution," The Wall Street Journal, June 29, 2014. http://on.wsj.com/2bCMHQD
[18] Casey B. Mulligan, The Redistribution Recession, pg. 38, 2012.

The Rejection of a "New Normal"

It is emblematic of economics that if government taxes production less and, at the same time, provides less compensation for those who don't work, there will be more output and less unemployment. Even Paul Krugman agrees (which should make me question its veracity):

> *Public policy designed to help workers who lost their jobs can lead to structural unemployment as an unintended side effect...The drawback to this generosity is that it reduces the incentive to quickly find a new job, and by keeping more people searching for longer, the benefits increase structural and frictional unemployment.[19]*

Each and every one of us knows that if our incentives increase we'll work harder, longer and smarter. If you don't believe me just compare employees at the Post Office or the Department of Motor Vehicles to entrepreneurs in businesses where pay corresponds to actual production. Work is a lot more fun with lower tax rates.

To show how important productivity is for economic growth, I have plotted productivity changes in the U.S. for the forty years from 1975 through 2016. Increases in overall productivity is a basic measure of the incentive effects on work, output and employment.

Productivity as Measured by Real Output Per Hour of All Persons
(1Q-75 to 2Q-16, quarterly, 2-year moving avg., % change at annual rate)

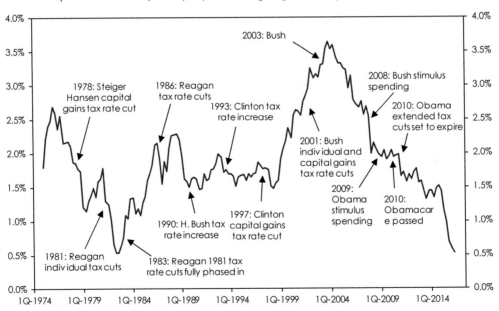

Source: Bureau of Labor Statistics

Many mainstream economists conclude that this period of extremely low and declining productivity gains is "the new normal," as seen in the figure above. It's not a new normal at all! Low productivity

---

[19] Paul Krugman and Robin Wells, Economics, Second Edition, Worth Publishers, 2009.

24

gains are exactly what happens when economic incentives are muted. Pro-growth policies on the other hand heighten incentives, which have positive effects on productivity growth that in turn generate a lot more jobs, output and employment. And with this type of GDP growth, tax revenues won't be a problem.

Putting productivity growth together with increases in employment, you'll be able to visualize what could and should happen. We know from the historical record above that the United States economy is capable of much more.

The Welfare Cliff: Why Would Anyone Want to Jump?

Stupid is as stupid does.
— Forrest Gump in the movie of the same name

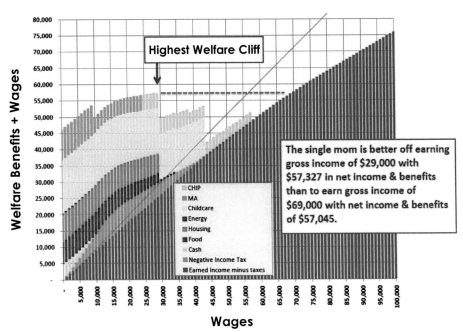

Source: American Enterprise Institute

The above chart shows total net spending power (the vertical axis) for a single woman in 2012 in Philadelphia with two children versus her total gross wages (the horizontal axis). Total net spending power includes all after-tax wages plus net welfare benefits that woman would be eligible for given her wages. As is the case with welfare benefits, they are subject to needs and/ or income tests. Thus, as the woman's wages rise, the welfare benefits hit cliffs where they are eliminated. The above chart shows a number of these cliffs.

As is clear from the chart, there are ranges of earned wages where the effective tax or disincentive effects exceed 100%. Who would ever want to earn more if your actual spending power dropped?

The most immoral act government can perpetrate on its citizenry is to enact policies that have the effect of destroying the production base from whence all beneficence ultimately flows.

The Welfare Trap Problem

Way back in 1978, Dr. Laffer documented the same phenomena (Los Angeles Times, Aug 20, 1978) in his article "Disincentives Drag Non-Whites Lower."

"In the persistent effort to achieve parsimony in conjunction with fairness and equity, social welfare programs have adopted stringent criteria for welfare recipients. For Social Security Recipients there is the "retirement" test which reduces the tax-free benefits allowed as earned income for the retired rises above $4,000 per year. Similar "means and income" test strictures apply to recipients of food stamps, housing subsidies, aid for dependent children, unemployment compensation, etc. These criteria of eligibility were designed to ensure that only the truly needy would receive the help they so desperately lacked." ….

"While these "means," "retirement," "incomes," "unemployment," and other "needs" tests may be rationalized on both moral and budget grounds, they have markedly perverse effects on the economic incentives of the poor." ….
"The net effects on spendable income of the combination of "needs" tests and taxes for inner-city family of four in Los Angeles are show in the table." …. (see table below)

"The impact of incremental increases in gross wages of 100 per month has been calculated up to $1,000 per month." ….

"Over the entire range from no wages to $1,000 per month…the family has at its disposal an additional $140.25 per month. This corresponds to an average tax "wedge" of 86%. For incomes between $400 and $800 per month, the family's ability to buy goods and services actually falls the more it earns. This corresponds to marginal tax rates of more than 100%." ….

"Individuals respond to incentives. People do not work for fun, nor do firms produce as a matter of social conscience." ….

"The good intentions of our social architects have all but eliminated economic incentives for one of our most disadvantaged groups—inner-city inhabitants. Until incentives are restored the prognosis for this sector of our economy and society remains bad however much is spent." …. Experience, it would seem, is the ability to recognize a mistake when you make it again.

A Look at the Poverty Trap (1978)
How the loss of welfare benefits and the bite of taxes reduces the incentive to work

Monthly Gross Wages	Net Family Spendable Income	Increase in Spendable Income	De Facto Marginal Tax Rate
0	$718.33	-	-
100	$759.43	$41.10	58.9%
200	$780.53	$21.10	78.9%
300	$810.57	$30.04	70.0%
400	$815.80	$5.23	94.5%
500	$794.58	$-21.22	121.2%
600	$794.58	$0	100.0%
700	$794.58	$0	100.0%
800	$809.92	$15.34	84.7%
900	$832.49	$22.57	77.4%
1,000	$858.58	$26.09	73.9%

Getting a Job Barely Paid in Obama's America

Paraphrasing President John F. Kennedy—*"No American can ever be made better off by pulling a fellow American down, and every American is made better off if any one of us is better off."* The line that President Kennedy said next was used in the Reagan campaign of 1980: *"A rising tide lifts all boats."* A growing economy is the best antidote for poverty, for despair, for inequity, as well as for many other afflictions of the human condition.

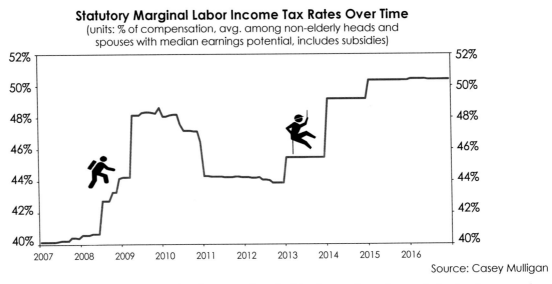

Statutory Marginal Labor Income Tax Rates Over Time
(units: % of compensation, avg. among non-elderly heads and spouses with median earnings potential, includes subsidies)

Source: Casey Mulligan

The climbing marginal income tax rates in the above graph truly drive home the point made in the above graph: as tax rates increase to fund ever expanding entitlement programs, the middle class is being squeezed thin.

Effective marginal tax rates, shown here for average earners,[20] take into account personal and payroll tax rates and government benefits that have to be given up when income rises. These effective tax rates have increased dramatically under President Obama.

This graph shows how an average earner—someone making median income in the US—faces, in real terms, far higher than the 10%, 15%, or 25% rates of the income tax such an earner would ordinarily be subject to. Because housing assistance, child tax credits, unemployment insurance and Obamacare subsidies phase out with income, the real loss to earning more at median income is over 50%.

One of the reasons this jobless recovery has been so weak is that getting a job in America these days barely pays. It is now sometimes more lucrative to stay on government benefits than it is to get a job. For a related chart, see "Highest Welfare Cliff" on page 26.

> *The best form of welfare is still a good, high-paying job.*
> — *President John F. Kennedy*

---

[20] Casey Mulligan, "Average Marginal Labor Income Tax Rates Under the Affordable Care Act," National Bureau of Economic Research, August 2013. http://www.nber.org/papers/w19365

Government Can and Has Gotten It Right Many Times—Part I

HITTING ON ALL FORTY-EIGHT

1950s cartoon promoting the new Interstate System with roadmap on the fender. Source: U.S. Department of Transportation

I-55 under construction in Mississippi, 1972. Source: U.S. National Archives and Records

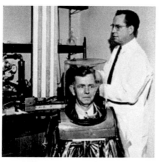

Scientists at USC research ways to cope with smog in the 1940s. Source: USC archives.

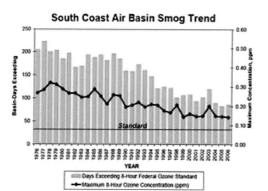

Source: Southern Coast AQMD

Example #1:

The Interstate Highway Program

• The Problem: The abundance of unsafe roads, inefficient routes and traffic jams that were limiting the nation's economic growth potential and its ability to respond to national security threats.

• The Solution: Though plans for a national highway system had been discussed by President Franklin Roosevelt as far back as 1936, it wasn't until Congress passed President Eisenhower's Federal-Aid Highway Act of 1956, that words became action.[21] The Federal government agreed to pay 90% of the cost of the Interstate System but left much decision making in the hands of the states. The Interstate System ended up costing $425 billion in 2006 dollars and was completed in 1992—with 200,733 miles. [22, 23]

Example #2:

Clearing the Smog in Los Angeles

• The Problem: In 1943, Los Angeles documented its first cases of smog.[24] The smog, which scientists tied to automobile use, made irritated eyes, irritated respiratory tracts, chest pains, cough, nausea and headaches a regular occurrence and led to long-term lung damage.

• The Solution: In 1947, L.A. started the Air Quality Management District (AQMD) and began monitoring smog levels. The AQMD passed rules limiting emissions from cars, factories and farms (often tires were burned to keep crops warm). The guidelines were enormously successful in reducing smog levels (see chart to the left). A 2016 study found smog reduction was critical to improving the health of children in Southern California. [25]

[21] U.S Department of Transportation
[22] Al Neuharth, "Traveling Interstates is our Sixth Freedom". USA Today. (June 22, 2006).
[23] U.S Department of Transportation
[24] "History of Smog," LA Weekly, Sept, 2005. http://www.laweekly.com/news/history-of-smog-2140714
[25] "SoCal's reduction in smog linked to major improvement in children's respiratory health

And the example that made all of these other great achievements possible:

Example #3:

U.S. Entry into World War I and World War II

We'll leave it to historians to explain the causes and consequences of WWI and WWII. But it is an uncontestable fact that the decision by the United States to enter into both wars was crucial to the victory of the Allied Powers and to the preservation of democracy and Western values. Furthermore, even under wartime controls, the U.S. economy demonstrated the productive superiority of the market system to the centrally planned economies of its enemies.

Housing Affordability: How the Fed Killed the Housing Market
The American Dream of Home Ownership Has Fallen to a 50-year Low

A fact without a theory is like a ship without a sail. Is like a boat without a rudder. Is like a kite without a tail. A fact without a theory is as sad as sad can be. But if there's one thing worse in this universe, it's a theory...without a fact.
— *George P. Shultz upon Milton Friedman's 90th birthday, 2001*

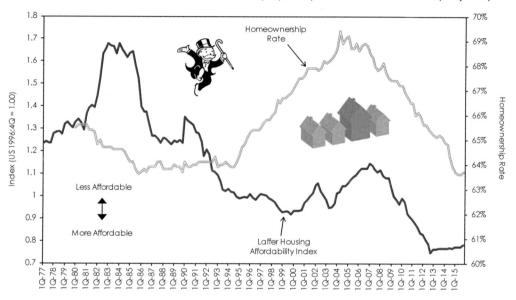

Laffer Housing Affordability Index vs. U.S. Homeownership Rate
(Index: quarterly, 1Q-1977 to 4Q-2015; Homeownership: quarterly, 1Q-80 to 4Q-15, seasonally-adjusted)

Source: Census Bureau, Laffer Associates

The Laffer Housing Affordability Index measures a typical mortgage payment for a median house relative to after-tax, median family income, allowing for 3-year rolling window of refinancing and capital gains appreciation of home value.

Overlapping the affordability index with the homeownership rate, the homeownership rate was at a 50-year low in 2015. It hit its all-time high just following President Clinton's term in office. What is so noticeable is that homeownership and affordability moved in opposite directions until early in President George W. Bush's term in office. The higher mortgage interest payments are, the more homeownership rates go down. But in the latest period covered, the circumstances are different. Most recently the lower interest rates are, the lower homeownership is.

To see why this happens, imagine a demand curve and a supply curve plotted against price (the vertical axis) and quantity (the horizontal axis). The two curves intersect at price P* and quantity Q*. Together, supply and demand determine price and quantity. As noted by Professor Alfred

Marshall, 125 years ago price and quantity are always determined by both together not either separately.[26]

In 2008, the Fed started to manipulate interest rates by intervening in the bond markets through quantitative easing and Operation Twist. The demand—infatuated Fed literally forced interest rates (i.e. prices) to be way below where they would have been in a free market.

If prices are pushed lower, below the equilibrium price of P*, demand would be higher and supply would be lower. With supply and demand no longer in equilibrium, you need a theory of the allocation of frustrations in order to determine whether the new price and quantity will lie on the supply curve or on the demand curve. As linear programmers know, the adjustment stops at the first constraint (the supply curve) and quantity will tumble. Which is exactly what it did.

Pushing interest rates down below equilibrium reduces the quantity of funds supplied to the housing market. And even though demanders want to borrow more, suppliers are unwilling to supply as much. Said differently, who in their right mind would want to lend to a risky homebuyer with a 30-year fixed-rate mortgage at 3%? No one! Interest rates that are too low destroy the housing production market.

---

[26] Alfred Marshall, Principles of Economics, Book 5, Chapter 3. 1890.

Your Home is Your Castle

Excessive taxation…extinguishes both production and consumption, and the taxpayer into the bargain…The diminution of demand must be followed by a diminution of the supply of production; and, consequently, of the articles liable to taxation.[27]
— *Jean-Baptiste Say, A Treatise on Political Economy, 1851*

New Home Sales Per 1,000 Adults vs. Employment to Population Ratio vs. 10-Year Treasury Yield
(monthly, Jan-63 to Sep-16, Treasury: eop)

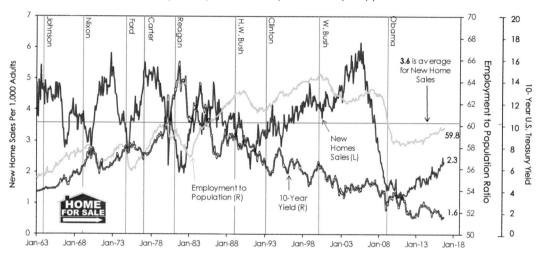

Source: Bloomberg, Bureau of Labor Statistics, Census Bureau

When President Reagan took office, the index of new home sales per 1,000 adults per year was significantly below its long-term mean and quickly rose above that mean. When President Reagan left office, new home sales were just about equal to the long-term mean. If new home sales were equal to their long term average of 3.6 per 1,000 adults per year, instead of the current reading of 2.3, the total number of new home sales in 2016 would have been 321,728 higher.

Under President Obama, new home sales per 1,000 adults per year has remained at all-time lows for the entire period of his presidency. But here's the spin: suppliers don't want to supply mortgage capital to home buyers when interest rates are too low and potential home buyers can't afford a home when jobs disappear.

We know it's hard for politicians and regulators to understand, but interest rates can be too high and therefore stifle the demand for homes. But interest rates can also sometimes be too low and stifle the supply of capital to the housing market. Whether interest rates are too high or too low,

---

[27] Bruce Bartlett, "Supply-Side Economics: 'Voodoo Economics' or Lasting Contribution?" Laffer Associates, November 11, 2003.

the housing market suffers. To paraphrase Charlton Heston in The Planet of the Apes, regulators should keep their stinking monkey paws off our economy.

> *We are poised for progress. Two years after the worst recession most of us have ever known, the stock market has come roaring back. Corporate profits are up. The economy is growing again.*[28]
> — *President Barack Obama, 2011 State of the Union*

[28] "Remarks by the President in State of Union Address," The White House, January 25, 2011. https://www.whitehouse.gov/the-press-office/2011/01/25/remarks-president-state-union-address

Weaving the Tapestry of the Big Lie with Threads of Partial Truths

In other words, it is not in the power of any human being to devise legislation or administration by which each man shall achieve success and have happiness; it not only is not in the power of any man to do that, but if any man says that he can do it, distrust him as a quack.[29]
— *Theodore Roosevelt, 1905*

Real Median Household Income
(annual, 2014 CPI-U Adjusted, semi-log scale, extrapolated: 1960-1978, actual: 1978-2015)
* Real household prior to 1978 was extrapolated using real family income data series

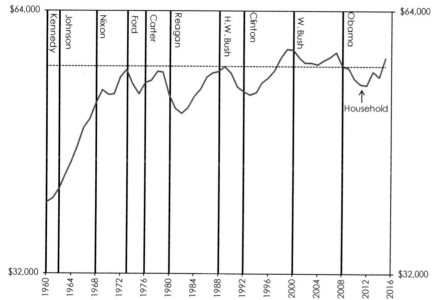

Year	Annualized Growth %
1961-1963	3.08%
1963-1969	3.86%
1969-1974	0.31%
1974-1977	0.29%
1977-1981	-1.80%
1981-1989	1.38%
1989-1993	-1.87%
1993-2001	1.23%
2001-2009	-0.35%
2009-2015	0.46%

Source: Census Bureau

Growth in median real household income is yet another measure of the success or failure of economic policies. This series measures the median income a household actually receives after accounting for inflation. The Census Bureau defines a household as consisting of one or more individuals living in the same unit, while a family consists of two or more individuals related by birth, marriage, or adoption.

The period including President Kennedy on through the first term of President Nixon's time in office was a smashing success. From 1961 through 1974, real median household income rose at an average annual rate of 2.34%. And why? President Kennedy cut the corporate tax rate (52% to 48%), the highest personal income tax rate (91% to 70%), cut tariffs by 35%, put in the 7% Investment Tax Credit and shortened the depreciable lives of plant equipment expenditures. In his first term in office, President Nixon cut the highest tax rate on earned income from 70% to 50%.

---

[19] Theodore Roosevelt, Works, p. 321, June 6, 1905.

But, then we get to Presidents Ford and Carter, with their anti-growth policies and the failure of median real household income to continue rising. From 1974 through 1981, growth in median real household income fell at an annualized rate of -0.91%.

Under President Reagan, with the major tax cuts, sound money and deregulation, growth in median real household income hit a 1.38% per annum average for 1981 through 1989. There was a negative lull under President George H.W. Bush after his tax increase, with growth averaging -1.87% per annum. But once President Clinton took office, growth in median real household income surged to 1.23% per annum. For the period 2001-2015 under Presidents George W. Bush and Barack Obama, with stimulus spending, bad monetary policies, and increased regulations, real median household income was essentially flat at an average annual rate of -0.002%.

Drugs have destroyed many lives, but wrongheaded governmental policies have destroyed many more.[30]
— Kofi Annan, 2016

---

[30] Kofi Annan, "Kofi Annan on Why It's Time To Legalize Drugs," The Global Commission on Drug Policy, February 22. 2016. http://www.globalcommissionondrugs.org/22-february-2016-lift-the-ban-kofi-annan-on-why-its-time-to-legalize-drugs/

The Greatest Story Never Told—Stephen Moore

I take it that it is best for all to leave each man free to acquire property as fast as he can. Some will get wealthy. I don't believe in a law to prevent a man from getting rich; it would do more harm than good.
—Abraham Lincoln, 1860

S&P 500 Index: Real and Nominal Price Returns
Monthly, Period: Jan-60 to Oct-16, semi-log, Jan-66=100, last data point eop

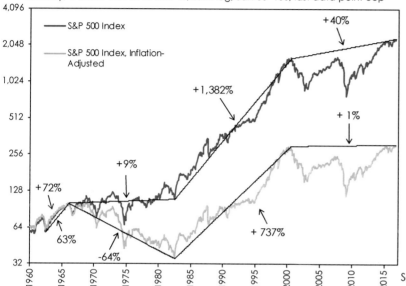

ANNUALIZED PRICE RETURNS (GROSS)**		
S&P 500 Index	Nominal	Real
Jun-62 to Present	6.7%	2.2%
Jun-62 to Jan-66	16.3%	14.6%
Jan-66 to Jul-82	0.5%	-6.1%
Jul-82 to Aug-00	16.1%	12.5%
Aug-00 to Oct-16	2.1%	0.0%
DJIA Index	Nominal	Real
Jun-62 to Present	5.9%	1.8%
Jun-62 to Jan-66	17.3%	15.6%
Jan-66 to Jul-82	-1.5%	-7.9%
Jul-82 to Aug-00	16.0%	12.4%
Aug-00 to Oct-16	3.0%	0.9%
**Returns calculated from intra-month highs/lows.		

Source: S&P, Bloomberg, Bureau of Labor Statistics

The above chart and table show nominal and real stock prices (S&P 500 and the Dow Jones Industrial Average) from 1960 to the present on a semi-log scale. The horizontal axis of the graph is time and is not in log form, but the vertical axis, which is stock prices, is in log form. What semi-log shows is that the slope of the stock price line over time represents the percentage growth in stock prices (rather than the less meaningful absolute dollar growth).

What should astound the reader is the huge rise in stock prices both nominal and real starting with President Kennedy from June 1962 to January 1966 and President Reagan from August 1982 on through President Clinton. Also, the abominable performance under Presidents Johnson, Nixon, Ford and Carter (-7.9% per annum compounded from January 1966 to July 1982 for the inflation-adjusted Dow Jones Industrial Average). The October 2016 inflation-adjusted S&P 500 Index is practically the same as it was in August of 2000. This is as good a representation of the market's view of economic policies as there is.

Kennedy further reiterated his beliefs in his Tax Message to Congress on January 24, 1963:

In short, this tax program will increase our wealth far more than it increases our public debt. The actual burden of that debt—as measured in relation to our total output—will decline. To continue to increase our debt as a result of inadequate earnings is a sign of weakness. But to borrow prudently in order to invest in a tax revision that will greatly increase our earning power can be a source of strength.[31]

But then there's always pearls of wisdom from Paul Krugman:

It really does now look like President Donald J. Trump, and markets are plunging. When might we expect them to recover? Frankly, I find it hard to care much, even though this is my specialty. The disaster for America and the world has so many aspects that the economic ramifications are way down my list of things to fear. Still, I guess people want an answer: If the question is when markets will recover, a first-pass answer is never.
— Paul Krugman, at 12:42 am Nov. 9th, the morning after Donald Trump was elected President. Dow Futures were down as much as 800 points at the time, before recovering most of their losses by 8am that same morning.[32]

[31] Arthur B. Laffer and Ford M. Scudder, "The Onslaught From the Left, Part II: Presidential Politics," Laffer Associates, January 25, 2008.
[32] https://www.nytimes.com/interactive/projects/cp/opinion/election-night-2016/paul-krugman-the-economic-fallout

Helicopter Ben

We must have a good definition of Money,
For if we do not, then what have we got,
But a Quantity Theory of no-one-knows what,
And this would be almost too true to be funny.
Now, Banks secrete something, as bees secrete honey;
(It sticks to their fingers, some even when hot!)
But what things are liquid and what things are not,

Rests on whether the climate of business is sunny.
For both Stores of Value and Means of Exchange
Include among Assets a very wide range,
So your definition's no better than mine.
Still, with credit-card-clever computers it's clear
That money as such will one day disappear;
Then, what isn't there we won't have to define.[33]
— *Kenneth Boulding, 1980*

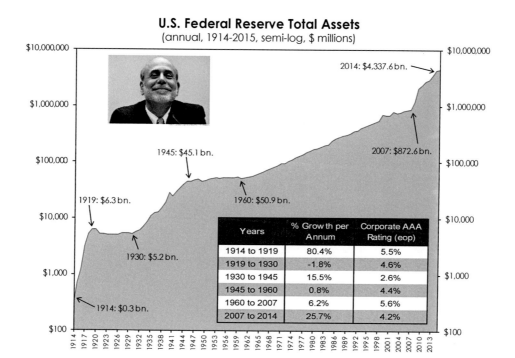

U.S. Federal Reserve Total Assets
(annual, 1914-2015, semi-log, $ millions)

2014: $4,337.6 bn.

1945: $45.1 bn.

2007: $872.6 bn.

1919: $6.3 bn.

1960: $50.9 bn.

1930: $5.2 bn.

1914: $0.3 bn.

Years	% Growth per Annum	Corporate AAA Rating (eop)
1914 to 1919	80.4%	5.5%
1919 to 1930	-1.8%	4.6%
1930 to 1945	15.5%	2.6%
1945 to 1960	0.8%	4.4%
1960 to 2007	6.2%	5.6%
2007 to 2014	25.7%	4.2%

Sources: Census Bureau, Federal Reserve, Historical Statistics of the U.S.

Total assets of the U.S. Federal Reserve is the single best measure of U.S. monetary expansion. In this chart, there are several periods of very rapid monetary expansion to wit: 1914-1919, 1930-1945 and, most recently, 2007-2014. These periods of rapid monetary expansion correspond directly to depressed times or war.

Monetary expansion stimulates nominal money demand for goods, but, without rigidities or illusions to bite on, it does not lead to real expansion. But growth of real output raises real money demand and thus abets the absorption of real monetary expansion into the economy without inflation. Tax reduction increases employment and growth and this raises the demand for money and hence enables the Federal Reserve to supply additional real money balances to the economy without causing sagging interest rates associated with conditions of loose money. Monetary acceleration is inflationary, but tax reduction is expansionary when there is unemployment.[34]
— *Robert Mundell, 1971*

---

[33] Kenneth E. Boulding, Beasts, Ballads, and Bouldingisms, January 1, 1980.
[34] Bruce Bartlett, "Supply-Side Economics: 'Voodoo Economics' or Lasting Contribution?" Laffer Associates, November 11, 2003.

Section III – Government Policy Actions: Stimulus Spending

I have concluded that the only effective way to restrain government spending is by limiting government's explicit tax revenue—just as a limited income is the only effective restraint on any individual's or family's spending.[35]
— Milton Friedman, Newsweek, 1978

In 2008, the U.S. Congress passed several stimulus packages, which were signed into law by President Bush. And then, once President Obama took office, yet another massive stimulus spending package was enacted. The idea is simple enough—according to the Keynesian narrative, just have the government write everyone what is called a refundable tax rebate check, and those rebate recipients will spend most of the money and create enough demand to employ some additional workers. And those additional workers, in turn, will spend more and so on down the line. If the original checks are large, ultimately the full effect will pull the economy out of its slowdown.

Yet, in this world of ours, those resources going to the refundable tax rebate recipients don't come from the Tooth Fairy. They come from workers and producers. If the resources come from workers and producers who thereby receive less for their work than they otherwise would have received, they will in turn spend less, and the people who now supply them with less will also spend less, and so on down the line in the opposite direction. As our former colleague and friend Milton Friedman liked to say, "There's no such thing as a free lunch."

The net effect is that the reduction in demand from those who fund the refundable tax rebate

[35] Bruce Bartlett, "Supply-Side Economics: 'Voodoo Economics' or Lasting Contribution?" Laffer Associates, November 11, 2003.

will be exactly the same size as the increase in demand from the tax rebate recipients. The income effects always net to zero.

All of the stimulative effects of the refundable tax rebate to the recipients will be 100% offset by the destimulative effects of the increase in liabilities of the workers and producers who have to pay for the transfer of resources to the rebate recipients. And even though the income effects net to zero, the substitution effects accumulate, and they accumulate in a most unpleasant way (see page 19). Any rebate will reduce output because it reduces everyone's incentives to produce output.[36]

Stimulus spending is one reason why we had the Great Depression and the Great Recession.

Over the past decades we've talked of curtailing government spending so that we can then lower the tax burden. Sometimes we've even taken a run at doing that. But there were always those who told us that taxes couldn't be cut until spending was reduced. Well, you know, we can lecture our children about extravagance until we run out of voice and breath. Or we can cure their extravagance by simply reducing their allowance.[37]
— President Ronald Reagan, 1981

You cannot legislate the poor into freedom by legislating the wealthy out of freedom. What one person receives without working for, another person must work for without receiving. The government cannot give to anybody anything that the government does not first take from somebody else. When half of the people get the idea that they do not have to work because the other half is going to take care of them, and when the other half gets the idea that it does no good to work because somebody else is going to get what they work for, that my dear friend, is about the end of any nation. You cannot multiply wealth by dividing it.
— Dr. Adrian Rogers, 1931

[36] Arthur B. Laffer, "That 'Stimulus' Nonsense," The Wall Street Journal, February 13, 2008.
http://www.wsj.com/articles/SB120286935977964221
[37] Bruce Bartlett, "'Starve the Beast': Origins and Development of a Budgetary Metaphor," Laffer Associates, June 26, 2007.

Government Spending is Taxation"—Milton Friedman

If someone says, "I'm from the government and I'm here to help you"—Run!

Government Spending as a Share of GDP vs. Unemployment Rate
(quarterly, 1Q-70 to 3Q-16, spending is federal, state & local NIPA-basis, unemployment is avg. of monthly)

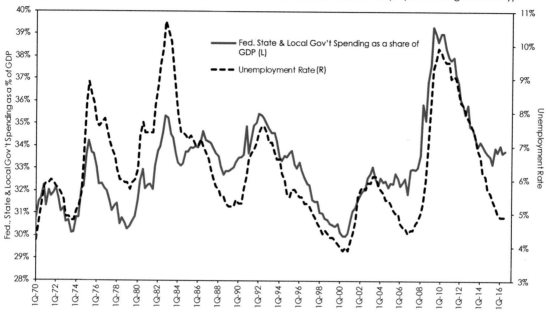

Source: Bureau of Economic Analysis, Bureau of Labor Statistics, Laffer Associates

University of Chicago Economics Professor, the late Milton Friedman, famously said that government spending is taxation, and as such if expanded too much, government spending hurts the economy. The chart above illustrates exactly what Professor Friedman meant.[38] There is as close to a perfect correlation between total government spending as a share of GDP and the unemployment rate as could be imagined. Far from helping the economy, government or stimulus spending actually hurts the economy. A country can't be taxed into prosperity, just as a poor person cannot spend him or herself into wealth.

If an economic theory is correct, it should be scalable, i.e. it should apply equally well to both small and large economies. Unfortunately, explaining correct theory in the context of a large economy is confusing, complicated and difficult to understand. In the limit, explaining correct economics in a very small economy is far easier to understand.

To see Professor Friedman's point simply and clearly, imagine a two-person world with only Farmer A and Farmer B—if Farmer B gets unemployment benefits, guess who pays for B's unemployment benefits? Correct, Farmer A pays for those benefits (i.e. the tax). Government

---

[38] Thank you to our friend Beau Duncan for first bringing this chart to our attention.

spending is taxation. Causation notwithstanding, the one thing we know is that as government spending increases, unemployment increases.

Now, gentlemen, we have tried spending money. We are spending more than we have ever spent before and it does not work. And I have just one interest, and if I am wrong, as far as I am concerned, somebody else can have my job. I want to see this country prosperous. I want to see people get a job. I want to see people get enough to eat...I say after eight years of this Administration we have just as much unemployment as when we started...And an enormous debt to boot![39]
— *Henry Morgenthau, Former U.S. Secretary of the Treasury of the Roosevelt Administration, 1939*

[39] "May 9, 1939," Henry Morgenthau Diary, Microfilm Roll #50, Franklin D. Roosevelt Library, Hyde Park, New York.
http://www.burtfolsom.com/wp-content/uploads/2011/Morgenthau.pdf

More Stimulus = Lower Growth

Government is not the solution, government is the problem.
— President Ronald Reagan, Inaugural Address, 1981

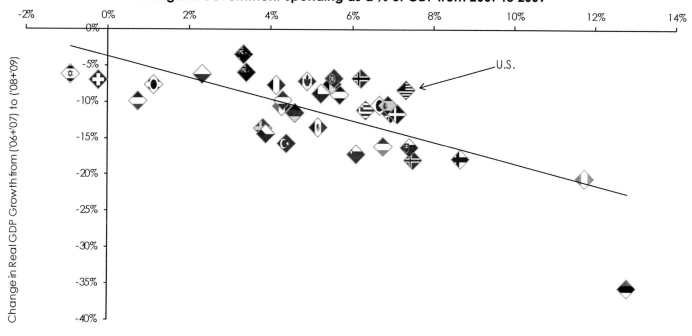

34 OECD Countries: Change in Real GDP Growth from (2006+2007) to (2008+2009) vs. Change in Government Spending as a % of GDP from 2007 to 2009

Source: OECD, IMF

Even if Milton Friedman is not your favorite modern economist (he's second from the top, just a smidgeon behind Nobel Prize winner Bob Mundell in our book), you've got to hand it to him when he reiterated time and again that government spending is taxation. This chart is yet another demonstration that government spending is taxation: a cross-section time series of the responses to the Great Recession, and subsequent consequences, by 34 member countries of the Organization for Economic Cooperation and Development (OECD), an international organization that aims to promote economic progress and world trade. These data are proof positive of just how right Milton Friedman was.

There is a clear and close inverse relationship between OECD countries' growth and their amount of stimulus spending. The more stimulus spending, the worse the growth. Q.E.D. (*Quod erat demonstrandum*, or which is what had to be shown).

45

I believe that there is a fundamental difference—and I think it has been evident in most of the answers that Mr. Carter has given tonight—that he seeks the solution to anything as another opportunity for a Federal Government program. I happen to believe that the Federal Government has usurped powers of autonomy and authority.[40]
— *Ronald Reagan, Carter–Reagan Presidential Debate, 1980*

[40] The Carter-Reagan Presidential Debate, October 28, 1980. http://www.debates.org/index.php?page=october-28-1980-debate-transcript

What Does $831 Billion Buy You? A Bad Economy
Caution: Some Academics Trade Principles for Power

Political economists rebut arguments they know to be true in order to curry favor with their political benefactors.

Unemployment Rate in Obama/Bernstein/Romer Stimulus Spending Forecast: Passed on Feb 17, 2009
(quarterly, Actual: 1Q-07 to 1Q-14, Forecasted With and Without Recovery as Published: 1Q-07 to 1Q-14)

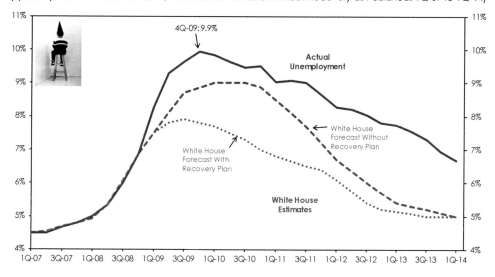

Source: Bureau of Labor Statistics, Romer and Bernstein (2009)

Professor Romer had a long career as an academic before taking a job for President Obama. In fact, here are some of her research findings as an academic as written in *The American Economic Review*:

> *"Our results indicate that tax changes have very large effects on output. Our baseline specification implies that an exogenous tax increase of one percent of GDP lowers real GDP by almost three percent."*[41]

Yet here is what she said as a political operative for President Obama in a document demanding the immediate implementation of a $¾ trillion government stimulus spending program:

> *"Even with the large prototypical package, the unemployment rate in 2010Q4 is predicted to be approximately 7.0%, which is well below the approximately 8.8% that would result in the absence of a plan."*[42]

As shown above, the actual unemployment rate in 4Q-2010 was well over 9% with the Obama stimulus package, as opposed to the 7% Professor Romer said it would be.

Would that she were aware of the words of Jean-Baptiste Say in 1834:

> *The encouragement of mere consumption is no benefit to commerce; for the difficulty lies in supplying the means, not in stimulating the desire of consumption…It is the aim of good government to stimulate production, of bad government to encourage consumption.*[43]

> *The curious task of economics is to demonstrate to men how little they really know about what they imagine they can design.*
> —*F.A. Hayek, The Fatal Conceit: The Errors of Socialism*

[41] Christina D. Romer and David H. Romer, "The Macroeconomic Effects of Tax Changes: Estimates Based on a New Measure of Fiscal Shocks" The American Economic Review, Vol. 100 No. 3, Pg. 799, June 2010. http://eml.berkeley.edu/~dromer/papers/RomerandRomerAERJune2010.pdf
[42] Christina Romer and Jared Bernstein, "The Job Impact of the American Recovery and Reinvestment Plan," January 9, 2009. https://otrans.3cdn.net/ee40602f9a7d8172b8_ozm6bt5oi.pdf
[43] Bruce Bartlett, "Supply-Side Economics: 'Voodoo Economics' or Lasting Contribution?" Laffer Associates, November 11, 2003.

Section IV – Government Policy Actions: Tax Rates and Income Tax Avoidance

Revenue estimates have a way of being very, very far off base because of the failure to anticipate everything that happens…Now, when we put the investment tax credit on, we estimated that we were going to lose about $5 billion…Instead of losing money, revenues went up in corporate income tax collections. Then we thought it was overheating the economy. We repealed it. We thought that the government would take in more money. But instead of making $5 billion, we lost $5 billion. Then, after a while, we thought we made a mistake, so we put it back on again. Instead of losing us money, it made us money. Then, after a while, we repealed it again and it did just exactly the opposite from what it was estimated to do again by about the same amount. It seems to me, if we take all factors into account, we wind up with the conclusion that taking the investment tax credit alone and looking at it by itself, it is not costing us any money. Because the impression I gain from it is that it stimulated the economy to the extent, and brings about additional investment to the extent, that it makes us money rather than loses us money.[44]
—*Senator Russell Long (D-LA), Chairman of the Senate Finance Committee, 1977*

In short, it is a paradoxical truth that tax rates are too high today and tax revenues are too low and the soundest way to raise the revenues in the long run is to cut the rates now.
—*John F. Kennedy, Address to the Economic Club of New York, December 14, 1962*

---

[44] Bruce Bartlett, "Supply-Side Economics: 'Voodoo Economics' or Lasting Contribution?" Laffer Associates, November 11, 2003.

The Laffer Curve

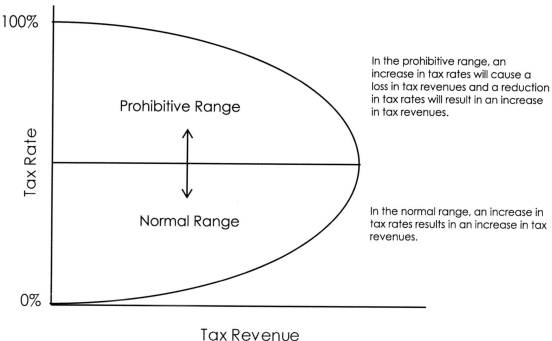

In the prohibitive range, an increase in tax rates will cause a loss in tax revenues and a reduction in tax rates will result in an increase in tax revenues.

In the normal range, an increase in tax rates results in an increase in tax revenues.

Dear Professor Laffer:

It is obvious that you read your press notices with some care; I am delighted not only by the way you accept my designation as an alternative source of essential public services but also by your good humour. I thank you very much for the fire engine; in due course I am sure my grandchildren will be no less grateful. As to my response, I am promptly initiating a search for a silver or gold-plated wishbone which is the nearest known approximation to the Laffer Curve. This I will hope to have in the mail to you in due course. Whether you get it or not will, of course, depend on whether the postal service survives your policies.

My thanks and cordial good wishes once again.

Yours faithfully,
John Kenneth Galbraith

March 1979[45]

[45] John Maynard Keynes, "Keynes and the Laffer Curve," Adam Smith Institute, January 4, 2011.
http://www.adamsmith.org/blog/tax-spending/keynes-and-the-laffer-curve

Scientific American and the Laffer Curve

In the early 1980s, the Laffer curve became a widely understood (and misunderstood!) economic tool and pop culture phenomenon. Below are excerpts from a 1981 article in the Scientific American, a widely read magazine in those days:

The supply-siders call themselves supply-siders in order to emphasize how they differ from neo-Keynesians. John Maynard Keynes stressed the importance of maintaining demand by minimum wage laws and welfare payments. The Lafferites turn this around and stress the importance of stimulating supply. With the government off the back of business, production will soar, new inventions will be made, more people will be employed and real wages will rise. Everyone benefits, particularly the poor, as prosperity trickles down from the heights (So far so good).

The trouble with the Laffer curve is that, like the Phillips curve, it is too simple to be of any service except as the symbol of a concept. In the case of the Laffer curve the concept is both ancient and trivially true, namely that when taxes are too high, they are counterproductive. The problem is how to define "too "high." (Hmm…)

Will the Lafferism of the Administration (The Republican Administration circa 1981) *succeed or will it, as many economists fear, plunge the nation into higher inflation and higher unemployment? The fact is economists cannot know* (Oh really?). *The technosnarl is too snarly. The idle rich might not invest their tax savings, as Lafferites predict but might spend it on increased consumption. The hardworking poor and middle class might decide to work less productively, not more. The corporations and conglomerates might do little with their tax savings except acquire other companies.* (What?)

Ideologues of all persuasions think they know exactly how the economy will respond to the Administration's mixture of Lafferism and monetarism. Indeed, their self-confidence is so vast, and their ability to rationalize so crafty, that one cannot imagine any scenario for the next few years they would regard as falsifying their dogma. (Even after Jimmy Carter?)

Will the president seek help from the zodiac in trying to decide whether to follow Friedman or Laffer or someone else? One may never know. As the Yale economist William Nordhaus put it (The New York Times, August 9): "We can only hope that supply-side economics turns out to be laetrile rather than thalidomide."

On the original Laffer curve:

Is it not a thing of beauty bare? As any child can see (true, any child can see this but almost no Ph.D. economists can) *from inspecting the curve's lower end, if the government drops its tax rate to nothing, it gets nothing. And if it raises its tax rates to 100 percent, it also gets nothing* (tell that to the CBO). *Why? Because in that case nobody will work for wages. If all income went to the state, people would revert to a barter economy in which a painter paints a dentist's house only if the dentist caps one of the painter's teeth.*

On Gardner's neo-Laffer (NL) curve (pictured on next page):

To bring Laffer's curve more into line with the complexities of a mixed economy dominated by what Galbraith likes to call the "technostructure," and also with other variables that distort the curve, I have devised what I call the neo-Laffer (NL) curve. (See my "Changing Perspectives on the Laffer Curve," in The British Journal of

Econometriciousness, Vol. 34, No. 8, pages 7316-7349; August 1980—(this is his joke not mine)). *The NL curve is shown in the lower illustration on this page. Observe that near its end points this lovely curve closely resembles the old Laffer curve, proving that it was not a totally worthless first approximation. As the curve moves into the complexities of the real world, however, it enters what I call the "technosnarl."*

And there you have it ladies and gentleman a scientific refutation of the Laffer Curve. Aren't scientists silly?

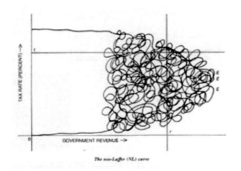

Source: Martin Gardner, "Mathematical Games: The Laffer curve and other laughs in current economics," The Scientific American, print edition, December 1981.

Government Can and Has Gotten It Right Many Times—Part II

Example #4: Preventing Species from Extinction

We do not know the true nature of the entity we are destroying.
—*Arthur C. Clarke, citing the large brain size of the blue whale in 1962*

Bald Eagle

In 1963, there were only 478 breeding pairs of bald eagles in the U.S. the species was on the verge of extinction due to deforestation, overhunting of prey, and the widespread use of the insecticide DDT, which caused eagles to lay eggs with thin shells that cracked before hatchlings were ready.[46]

Banning DDT, prohibiting the killing of bald eagles, improving water quality, protecting nest sites all served to boost the number of breeding pairs to just under 10,000 by 2006. The bald eagle was taken off the endangered species list in 2007. There were an estimated 10,000 breeding pairs of bald eagles in the contiguous U.S. as of 2006.[47]

Blue and Grey Whale

The blue whale is considered to be the largest animal on Earth (ever!), measuring between 82 and 105 ft. and weighing up to 200 tons. The blue whale typically lives 80-90 years, but some live much longer.

Prior to the 1860s, blue whales were too swift and powerful for hunters to kill, but the advent of harpoon cannons enabled hunters to capture them in large numbers. Between 1900 and 1965, some 360,000 blue whales were slaughtered, leaving them on the brink of extinction with a population of 1,000.[49] In 1966, the blue whale fell under the global protection of the International Whaling Commission. The blue whale remains an endangered species. There are an estimated 10,000-25,000 blue whales alive today.

American Bison

In the 16th century, 30-60 million bison roamed throughout North America.[50] The westward expansion of European settlers and Native Americans put pressure on bison populations over the next 300 years. Bison were hunted for their pelts and killed in large numbers to clear land for railroads.

In the 1870s, one railway company shipped 500,000 bison hides back to the East.[51] By 1889, a mere 1,000 living in the U.S. and Canada; the trade in bison hides ended. In the 1890s, states and the federal government took action to preserve the bison. Markets also played a role: the high market value of the remaining bison (695 sold for $170k in 1912) incentivized private preservation and breeding. While still on the endangered species list, the bison population is estimated at 500,000.[52]

Other Species Preserved through Government Action:

Blue and Grey Whale

After 42 years on the endangered species list, the Yellowstone grizzly bear—whose population has grown from 150 to 700—was taken off the list in 2017.

Florida Panther

In the 1970s, between 12 and 20 Florida Panthers lived in the wild; that population grew to between 100 and 160 by 2015. "Indeed, there are so many big cats in the Everglades that they are venturing out in search of new territory."
Source: *The New Yorker*

Peregrine Falcon

After dwindling to 324 nesting pairs in 1975, there are now between 2,000 and 3,000 nesting pairs of Peregrine Falcons in the United States.

Massasauga Rattler

The population of the only venomous snake found in the Great Lakes region has been steadily declining. Due to the difficulty in tracking the species, the current population is unknown.

[46] "Bald Eagles, Life History and Conservation Success," U.S. Fish & Wildlife Service. Updated on April 20, 2015. https://www.fws.gov/Midwest/eagle/recovery/index.html
[47] "Bald Eagle: Fact Sheet: Natural History, Ecology, and History of Recovery, U.S. Fish and Wildlife Service, https://www.fws.gov/midwest/eagle/population/index.html
[48] "Blue Whales," National Geographic, http://www.nationalgeographic.com/animals/mammals/b/blue-whale/
[49] "Blue Whale," The Marine Mammal Center," http://www.marinemammalcenter.org/education/marine-mammal-information/cetaceans/blue-whale.html
[50] https://www.fws.gov/bisonrange/timeline.html
[51] "Timeline of the American Bison," Smithsonian Institute, https://www.fws.gov/bisonrange/timeline.htm
[52] "Restoring North America's Wild Bison to Their Home on the Range," http://www.ens-newswire.com/ens/mar2010/2010-03-03-01.html

Buffett Pays Even Less Than He Admits

That is the beauty of this tax. Unlike the one we have now that has 4000 pages about as tall as this podium and none of those pages are for you and me, they're for people with a high priced lawyer who buy those loopholes.[53]
—Gov. Jerry Brown, 1992

The world's richest man, Warren Buffett, was honored by President Obama for supporting higher tax rates on the rich. Buffett was awarded the Presidential Medal of Freedom. Here is the true story of how Warren Buffett avoids paying his fair share of taxes.

In a New York Times op-ed in 2011, Warren Buffett wrote that he paid an average tax rate of only 17.4% in 2010, less than anyone in his office.[54] He wrote he paid $6,923,494 in taxes, which means Buffett's 2010 taxable income was $39.8 million ($6.923 / 17.4%).

This is misleading. Buffett's method of calculating his tax rate runs contrary to how you or we think of tax rates, which is taxes paid as a percentage of adjusted gross income (AGI). Buffett's self-reported tax rate of 17.4% looks at taxes as a percentage of taxable income, which is AGI minus any personal exemptions or itemized deductions. To actually compare apples to apples, we should look at Buffett's AGI, which, according Buffett's 2010 tax statement, was $62.86 million, meaning Buffett paid 11.06% of his AGI in taxes.[55]

In truth, Buffett made far more than $39.7 million taxable income, or $62.86 million AGI, in 2010. According to economists' definition of income, income is i.) what you spend, ii.) what you give away, and iii.) the increase in your wealth over a given period of time, usually one year. In 2010, Buffett's income by this measure was over $12 billion. Buffett successfully, and legally, shelters the vast majority of his true income from taxation. His principal sources of tax avoidance include: increases in unrealized capital gains for which there is no tax; buying and selling assets inside the Berkshire Hathaway corporate structure, where Buffett doesn't have to pay personal capital gains tax; Berkshire Hathaway being an insurance company, which means he can deduct future expected losses against current income and allows him to earn income on deferred taxes; tax-free gifts to friends' and relatives' tax exempt foundations; and a number of other tax loopholes where the gifts are 100% tax deductible.

Buffett's change in wealth for 2010 as measured by Forbes comprises the $10 billion increase in the value of Warren Buffett's holdings of Berkshire Hathaway stock plus the $1¾ billion he gave

---

[53] Gov. Jerry Brown, 1992 Presidential Election, Democratic Candidates Debate, March 15, 1992.

[54] Warren E. Buffett, "Stop Coddling the Super-Rich," The New York Times, August 14, 2011. http://www.nytimes.com/2011/08/15/opinion/stop-coddling-the-super-rich.html

[55] Janet Novack, "Warren Buffett's Effective Federal Income Tax Rate Was Just 11%" Forbes, October 12, 2011. http://www.forbes.com/sites/janetnovack/2011/10/12/warren-buffets-effective-federal-income-tax-rate-is-just-11/#40cb73b6132b

away to the Bill and Melinda Gates Foundation in 2010. Adding in the gifts to his son's and daughter's foundations plus, plus, plus, Warren Buffett's real income was well over $12 billion, and his tax rate wasn't 17.4%, it was 6/100ths of 1% ($6.9 million in taxes / $12 billion income), all legal and all shows just how corrupt our tax codes really are.

2010 Tax Rate: Warren Buffett vs. Average U.S. Taxpayer

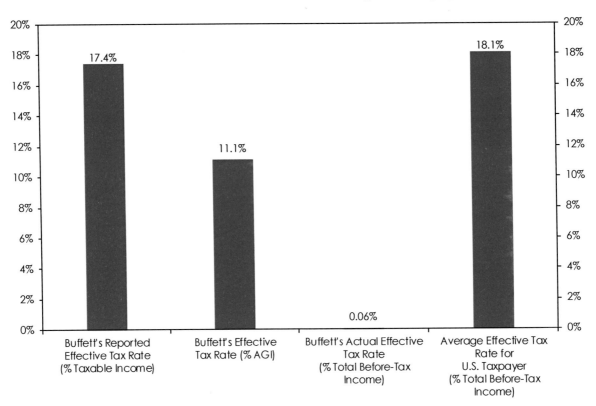

Source: Forbes, Laffer Associates, The New York Times, The Tax Foundation

We have a 4,000 page tax morass that feeds on the corruption of selling loopholes for campaign contributions.[56]
—Gov. Jerry Brown, 1992

---

[56] Gov. Jerry Brown, 1992 Presidential Election, Democratic Candidates Debate, March 1, 1992.

Bill Gates – Initiative 1098
Let Them Spend it All

In November of 2010, the state of Washington voted on Initiative 1098 – a tax the rich proposal targeted at adopting a brand new state income tax for high income earners.

This initiative would have imposed a new 5% tax on individuals earning over $200,000 per year and an additional 4% surcharge would be levied on individuals and couples earning more than $500,000 and $1 million, respectively. This was known as the Bill Gates initiative named after Bill Gates Sr. and probably his son too. The funds generated would have been directed to a fund for education and health services.

The pro taxers spent slightly more than those against the initiative, and yet the initiative was rejected 65% to 35%.

Enjoy my brief but poignant letter exchange with Bill Gates Sr.

December 5, 2006

Arthur Laffer
2909 Poston Avenue, 2nd Floor
Nashville, TN 37203

Dear Mr. Laffer:

Thank you for your recent mail enclosing the discussion (certainly NOT a debate) between you and Milton Friedman and the reprint of the Henninger article.

I have but little intellectual basis for doing so but nevertheless disagree wholeheartedly with the themes in this material. I just hold to the view that our greatest assets come from government supplied investments: education and research, for example. I worry about the inordinate political influence of rich people and the extraordinary multiplication of super wealthy families with impregnable wealth.

I am happy to be on your mailing list.

Sincerely,

William H. Gates

I'm not a macroeconomics person.
—Bill Gates Jr.

There are some ideas so absurd that only an intellectual could believe them.
—George Orwell

April 17, 2008

Arthur B. Laffer
Laffer Associates
2909 Poston Avenue, 2nd Floor
Nashville, TN 37203

Dear Arthur,

I have read all of the stuff you sent along with your letter of March 17.

I am not sure there is much to be said for a correspondence between us. I do not see any room for either of us to move in the direction of the other's philosophy.

I am a fan of progressive taxation. I would say our country has prospered from using such a system--even at 70% rates to say nothing of 90%.

It was nice of the RCG folks to provide the lunch and opportunity to hear your views.

Sincerely,

William H. Gates Sr.

Falling Tax Rates for the Rich Mean Greater Tax Revenues for America

The history of taxation shows that taxes which are inherently excessive are not paid. The high rates inevitably put pressure upon the taxpayer to withdraw his capital from productive business and invest it in tax-exempt securities or to find other lawful methods of avoiding the realization of taxable income. The result is that the sources of taxation are drying up; wealth is failing to carry its share of the tax burden; and capital is being diverted into channels which yield neither revenue to the Government nor profit to the people.
—Andrew Mellon, Taxation: The People's Business, 1924

The reason the Government is in deficit is because you have more than 4 million people unemployed, and because the last five years you have had rather a sluggish growth, much slower than any other Western country. I am in favor of a tax cut because I am concerned that if we don't get the tax cut that we are going to have an increase in unemployment and that we may move into a period of economic downturn. We had a recession in '58, a recession in 1960. We have done pretty well since then, but we still have over 4 million unemployed. I think this tax cut can give the stimulus to our economy over the next 2 or 3 years. I think it will provide for greater national wealth. I think it will reduce unemployment. I think it will strengthen our gold position. So I think that the proposal we made is responsible and in the best interests of the country...I think our whole experience in the late '50s shows us how necessary and desirable it is. My guess is that if we can get the tax cut, with the stimulus it will give to the economy, that we will get our budget in balance quicker than we will if we don't have it.
—John F. Kennedy, Interview on NBC's "Huntley-Brinkley Report," 1963

Tax Revenues as a Share of GDP for the Top 1% of Income Earners vs. Bottom 95% of Income Earners vs. Highest Marginal Tax Rate
(annual, 1916 to 2013)

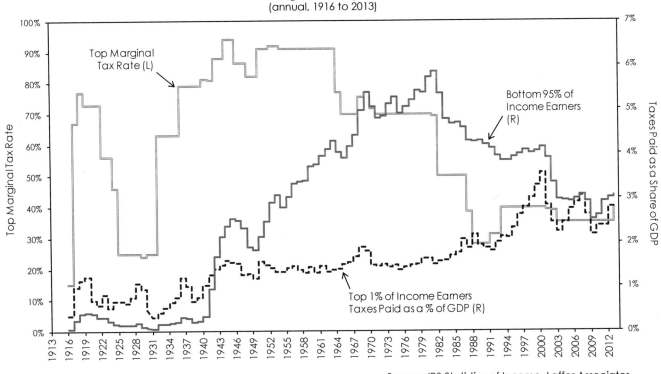

Source: IRS Statistics of Income, Laffer Associates

People earn income after tax to save and consume. The lower the tax rate, the more willing people are to work. After-tax income is the return on labor for the rich and poor alike.

Following the massive (Reagan) tax rate cuts of the 1980s, tax revenues from the top 1% of income earners have soared, while tax revenues from the bottom 95% of tax payers have tumbled. With President Obama's tax increases, all taxes have fallen. And the reason? The economy has collapsed because of anti-growth policies, hurting all groups.

The chart left shows that the tax revenues by the top 1% of income earners as a share of gross domestic product (GDP) rise when tax rates fall as often as they rise when tax rates rise. In fact, the whole period from 1963 (Kennedy) on is a perfect example of falling tax rates on the rich and increasing tax revenues from the rich.

If ever you questioned the Laffer Curve, just look at the left chart. This will make you a true believer.

> *The true crux of the taxation issue is to be seen in the paradox that the more taxes increase, the more they undermine the market economy and concomitantly the system of taxation itself…Every specific tax, as well as a nation's whole tax system, becomes self-defeating above a certain height of the rates.*[57]
> — *Ludwig von Mises, Human Action, 1949*

---

[57] Bruce Bartlett, "Supply-Side Economics: 'Voodoo Economics' or Lasting Contribution?" Laffer Associates, November 11, 2003.

One of These is Not Like the Other—Scott Grannis

Tax Rates vs. Tax Revenues
(annual, 1940-2016)

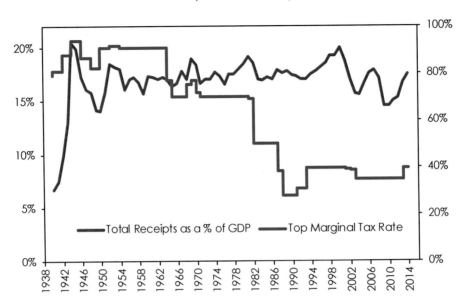

Source: Tax Policy Foundation, OMB

The emotional and divisive discussion of the top marginal income tax rate is as economically superfluous as it is damaging to our social fabric. Looking at historical tax rates, changes in the highest marginal income tax rate that have been enacted do not effect tax revenues in the manner those who favor increasing progressivity suggest they would.

In the chart above, you see the top marginal income tax rate changing dramatically over the years, all while total current receipts as a percent of GDP remains the same.

Higher tax bracket earners have more ways to avoid taxes than do lower income tax bracket earners, and they more often than not have the means as well as the ways to hire lawyers, accountants, deferred income specialists and other favor-grabbers to guide them into the ways of lowering their tax burden per dollar of income. Because of gimmicks, dodges, tax loopholes and the like, the elasticity of the supply of taxable income is the greatest in the highest income tax brackets. This isn't populism or elitism; it's economics.

That's not tax reform. That's just a tax giveaway to the very, very wealthy that will explode the deficit.[58]
— *Senator Charles Schumer, 2017*

The history of taxation shows that taxes which are inherently excessive are not paid. The high rates inevitably put pressure upon the taxpayer to withdraw his capital from productive business and invest it in tax-exempt securities or to find other lawful methods of avoiding the realization of taxable income. The result is that the sources of taxation are drying up; wealth is failing to carry its share of the tax burden; and capital is being diverted into channels which yield neither revenue to the Government nor profit to the people.[59]
—*Treasury Secretary Andrew Mellon*

Our true choice is not between tax reduction, on the one hand, and the avoidance of large Federal deficits on the other. It is increasingly clear that no matter what party is in power, so long as our national security needs keep rising, an economy hampered by restrictive tax rates will never produce enough revenues to balance our budget just as it will never produce enough jobs or enough profits... In short, it is a paradoxical truth that tax rates are too high today and tax revenues are too low and the soundest way to raise the revenues in the long run is to cut the rates now.[60]
— *President John F. Kennedy*

---

[58] Damian Paletta, "White House unveils dramatic plan to overhaul tax code," Washington Post, April 26 2017. https://bangordailynews.com/2017/04/26/news/nation/white-house-unveils-dramatic-plan-to-overhaul-tax-code/?ref=latest
[59] Daniel Mitchell, "The Historical Lessons of Lower Tax Rates," The Heritage Foundation, August 13 2003. https://www.heritage.org/node/18247/print-display
[60] Daniel Mitchell, "The Historical Lessons of Lower Tax Rates," The Heritage Foundation, August 13 2003. https://www.heritage.org/node/18247/print-display

The 20s, 60s and 80s: Tax Cuts Worked Throughout History

A sharp reduction in top tax rates below the present level of 91 percent would increase government revenues.[61]
—Henry Hazlitt, Newsweek column, 1954

There is no doubt in my mind that [the Kennedy] tax reduction bill, in and of itself, can bring about an increase in the gross national product of approximately $50 billion in the next few years. If it does, these lower rates of taxation will bring in at least $12 billion in additional revenue.[62]
—Wilbur Mills, 1963

Federal Tax Rate Cut/Federal Tax Revenue Growth and Real GDP Growth
(tax revenue growth before and after tax rate cuts are for the 4-year or 5-year period)

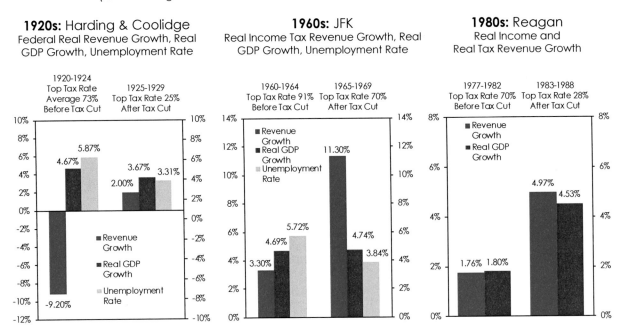

The three graphs above show the growth in inflation-adjusted federal tax revenues and growth in real GDP in the four years preceding the tax cut and the four years following the tax cut for the massive income tax rate cuts of the 1920s (Presidents Harding and Coolidge), the 1960s (President Kennedy) and the 1980s (President Reagan). In all three episodes of massive tax rate reductions, tax revenues grew much faster after the tax cuts than they had grown before the tax cuts. Supply-side economics and the Laffer curve are everywhere to be found.

When asked by Senator Jacob Javits (R-NY) before the Joint Economic Committee to comment on the assertion that Kennedy's tax cuts increased federal revenue, Walter Heller said:

---

[61] Bruce Barlett, "Laffer Curve Part 3," October 1, 2012. http://papers.ssrn.com/sol3/papers.cfm?abstract_id=2155979
[62] Bruce Bartlett, "Supply-Side Economics: 'Voodoo Economics' or Lasting Contribution?" Laffer Associates, November 11, 2003.

What happened to the tax cut in 1965 is difficult to pin down, but insofar as we are able to isolate it, it did seem to have a tremendously stimulative effect, a multiplied effect on the economy. It was the major factor that led to our running a $3 billion surplus by the middle of 1965, before escalation in Vietnam struck us. It was a $12 billion tax cut, which would be about $33 or $34 billion in today's terms. And within 1 year the revenues into the Federal Treasury were already above what they had been before the tax cut...Did it pay for itself in increased revenues? I think the evidence is very strong that it did. [63]

But then, when it came to the Reagan tax cuts of the 1980s, Walter Heller played a very different tune:

 In short, the Kemp-Roth enthusiasts rely excessively on post hoc, ergo propter hoc reasoning and on a one-dimensional view of the world. Have they forgotten that there is more to life than economic life, and that there is more to economics than taxes?...Nothing in the history of tax cuts, econometric studies of taxpayer responses, or field surveys of incentives suggests that the effects of a big tax cut on the supply of output even begin to match its effects on the demand for output. A $114 billion tax cut in three years would simply overwhelm our existing productive capacity with a tidal wave of increased demand and sweep away all hopes of curbing deficits and containing inflation. Indeed, it would soon generate soaring deficits and roaring inflation. [64]

But 1992 Presidential candidate Jerry Brown understood the power of tax reform:

I believe the number 1 step would be to clear away the underbrush of this 'disgrace to the human race' as President Carter called the tax code, and replace all the existing federal tax laws, corporate, personal income social security, gasoline tax... eliminate them and in their place put a flat tax. [65]

[63] Ibid.
[64] Walter Heller, "The Kemp-Roth-Laffer Free Lunch," in The Economics of the Tax Revolt, ed. Arthur B. Laffer & Jan P. Seymour, p. 48, 1979.
[65] Gov. Jerry Brown, 1992 Presidential Election, Democratic Candidates Debate, March 1, 1992.

Tax the Rich: The Harding/Coolidge Tax Cuts

John and Yoko Lennon

The Clarion Call of a Fabian Socialist:
Imagine no possessions
I wonder if you can
No need for greed or hunger
A brotherhood of man
Imagine all the people
Sharing all the world…

—*John Lennon, "Imagine"*

Vladimir Lenin

Perhaps most illustrative of the power of the Harding/Coolidge tax cuts was the increase in GDP, the fall in unemployment and the improvement in the average American's quality of life over the decade of the 1920s.

Percentage Share of Total Income Taxes Paid and Statutory Marginal Tax Rates By Income Class for Select Years

Income Class		1920	1925	1929	1920-1929 Change in Tax Share
Under $5,000	Tax Rate	8%	3%	3%	↓
	Tax Share	15.4%	1.9%	0.4%	
$5,000-$10,000	Tax Rate	11%	5%	5%	↓
	Tax Share	9.1%	2.6%	0.9%	
$10,000-$25,000	Tax Rate	19%	12%	12%	↓
	Tax Share	16.0%	10.1%	5.2%	
$25,000-$100,000	Tax Rate	56%	24%	24%	↓
	Tax Share	29.6%	36.6%	27.4%	
Over $100,000	Tax Rate	73%	25%	25%	↑
	Tax Share	29.9%	48.8%	62.2%	

Source: IRS

In regards to the 1920s, Historian Benjamin Rader concluded, *"Despite sharply reduced tax rates for upper income groups…the wealthy paid a larger share of the federal tax burden at the end of the decade than at the beginning."*[66] The evidence strongly indicates that the tax cuts of the 1920s did indeed raise revenue among those most affected by the rate reductions.

---

[66] Bruce Bartlett, "Supply-Side Economics: 'Voodoo Economics' or Lasting Contribution?" Laffer Associates, November 11, 2003.

But those income classes with lower tax rates were not left out in the cold: The Harding/ Coolidge tax-rate cuts did result in reduced tax rates on lower income brackets. Internal Revenue Service data show that the dramatic tax cuts of the 1920s resulted in an increase in the share of total income taxes paid by those making more than $100,000 per year from 29.9% in 1920 to 62.2% in 1929. And keep in mind the significance of this increase, given that the 1920s was a decade of falling prices and therefore a $100,000 threshold in 1929 corresponds to a higher real income threshold than $100,000 did in 1920. The consumer price index *fell* a combined 14.5% from 1920 to 1929. In this case, the effects of bracket creep that existed prior to the federal income tax brackets being indexed for inflation (in 1985) worked in the opposite direction.

Great	Greater	Greatest
Harding	Coolidge	Mellon

Though the marginal tax rates were cut much more for the highest income taxpayers, the effective burden of taxation shifted away from the lower-income taxpayers toward the higher-income taxpayers. The resulting decline in tax avoidance, in conjunction with economic growth, led to some increase in personal income tax receipts despite the huge tax cuts from 1921 through 1926. Thus, the tax rate cuts worked much as Mellon and other early "supply-side" supporters had argued that they would.[67]
—*Smiley and Keehn, 1995*

---

[67] Bruce Bartlett, "Supply-Side Economics: 'Voodoo Economics' or Lasting Contribution?" Laffer Associates, November 11, 2003.

Tax the Rich: The Kennedy Tax Cuts

Paul Krugman **Karl Marx** **Groucho Marx** **Bernie Sanders**

All animals are equal, but some animals are more equal than others.
— one of the Seven Commandments, Animal Farm

Percent Change in Taxes Paid and Percentage Point Change in Statutory Tax Rate by Income Class from 1963 (before Kennedy cut took effect) to 1966 (after the Kennedy tax cuts were in effect)

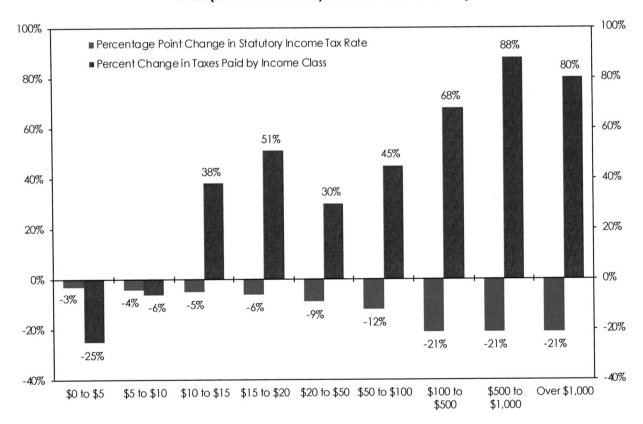

Income Level (000s)

Source: Joint Economic Committee

The point of the chart to the left is simply that, after the massive Kennedy tax cut, growth in tax revenues from higher income earners was a lot greater than growth in tax revenues from lower income earners.

President Kennedy shortened the depreciable lives for plant and equipment expenditures and enacted a 7% investment tax credit to increase business and personal incentives to save and invest. He also initiated radical accelerated depreciation to incentivize business investment.

President Kennedy reduced tariffs by some 35% in an international agreement carrying his name. Kennedy cut the highest corporate income tax rate from 52% to 48%. He had originally proposed cutting the corporate tax rate to 46%, but this was blocked by the Republicans led by Senator Barry Goldwater. President Kennedy also cut the highest marginal personal income tax rate from 91% to 70% and the lowest rate from 20% to 14% and all rates in between.

> *The main purpose of this paper is to demonstrate that not only may statutory and effective rates differ, but that it is distinctly possible on theoretical grounds that statutory rate increases may result in lower tax collections for some groups (i.e., lower effective rates). Furthermore, I submit that this perverse effect is most likely to occur among the rich, and it may even occur when work incentives are unaffected.*
> — *Richard McKenzie, 1973*

Tax the Rich: The Reagan Tax Cuts

- **•Unearned income tax**
  from 70% to 28%[68]

- **•Earned income tax**
  from 50% to 28%

- **•Corporate income tax**
  from 46% to 34%

•Capital gains tax from 39.95% to 28%.[69] **In 1997, the capital gains tax was eliminated on owner-occupied homes**

Chart A
Marginal Statutory Tax Rates and Effective Comprehensive Household Income Tax Rates: The Top 1%
(1980-1988)

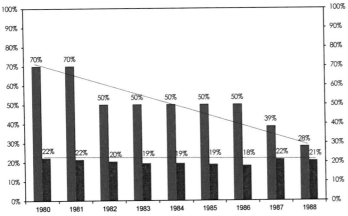

Comprehensive Income: This "measure includes all cash income (both taxable and tax-exempt), taxes paid by businesses (which are imputed to individuals), employees' contributions to 401(k) retirement plans, and the value of income received in kind from various sources (such as employer-paid health insurance premiums, Medicare and

Chart B
Percentage Point Change in Marginal Statutory Tax Rates And Percent Change in Number of Tax Returns by AGI Level
(1980-1988)

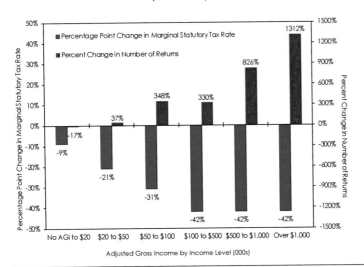

Chart A shows that while the highest statutory tax rate on the top 1% of income earners tumbles from 70% to 28%, their effective comprehensive income tax rate barely changes.

The effective comprehensive income tax rate is so stable while statutory tax rates on the rich bounce all over the place because the very highest income earners are able to change their reported income and thus control the amount of taxes they pay. Whether through tax shelters, deferrals, gifts, write-offs, income mobility over different types of income or any of a number of other measures, the effective comprehensive household income tax rate for the highest 1% of income earners barely budges.

One effect of lowering tax rates on the rich is that by doing so the number of rich filing taxes increases enormously. You can see in the chart to the right (chart B) that the number of tax returns filed between 1980 and 1988 increases sharply by the level of Adjusted Gross Income (AGI).

---

[68] Sources: "Historical Effective Federal Tax Rates", Congressional Budget Office, December 11, 2007 and IRS, Statistics of Income.
[69] This was cut in 1978 by the Steiger Hansen legislation signed in protest by President Carter.

Chart C
Dollar Change in Total Pre-Tax Comprehensive Income And Total Comprehensive Income tax Liability
(1980-1988)

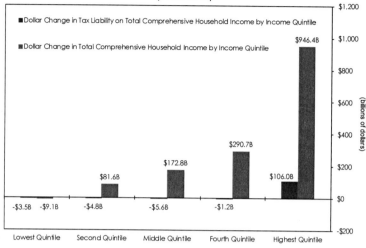

While statutory tax rates on the rich have fallen dramatically, total tax payments (and reported comprehensive income) have risen far more than any other income group.

The only conclusion one can come to is that by raising or lowering statutory tax rates on the rich, the effective individual income tax rate won't change, but the comprehensive household income earned by this group will either fall or rise dramatically. In other words tax revenues from the rich depend exclusively on the volume of income reported by the rich which itself increases with lower statutory tax rates.

If you want to get more tax revenues from the rich, you've got to make the rich richer, and to make the rich richer you've got to lower statutory tax rates on the rich. This is one era, for sure, where the Laffer curve thrives.

Don't Tax You, Don't Tax Me, Tax the Man Behind the Tree
—Russell Long

I just happen to believe that free enterprise can do a better job of producing the things that people need than government can.[70]
— *Ronald Reagan, Carter-Reagan Presidential Debate, 1980*

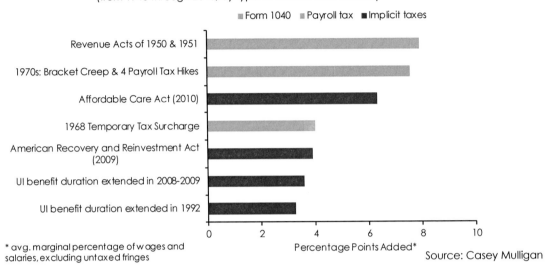

The Largest Marginal Labor Income Tax Rate Increases
(from 1946 through 2016, by type of federal tax increase)

* avg. marginal percentage of wages and salaries, excluding untaxed fringes

Percentage Points Added*

Source: Casey Mulligan

If you're old, you might remember all of these enormous tax increases, but whether you remember them or you're just too young, history tells you that these major tax increases preceded periods of slow growth and despair.[71] Additionally, what the graph shows us is that there have been three major tax rate increases in the past decade, yet only four tax rate increases in the preceding five decades.

There is a point at which in peace times high rates of income and profits taxes discourage energy, remove the incentive to new enterprise, encourage extravagant expenditures and produce industrial stagnation with consequent unemployment and other attendant evils.[72]
— *Woodrow Wilson, 1919*

It cannot be said too often—at any rate, it is not being said nearly often enough—that collectivism is not inherently democratic, but, on the contrary, gives to a tyrannical minority such powers as the Spanish Inquisitors never dreamed of.
— *George Orwell in his review of The Road to Serfdom, 1944*

For 25 years, virtually every bipartisan budget deal has meant higher taxes, higher spending and political carnage for the GOP.
— *Stephen Moore, The Wall Street Journal, 2006*

[70] The Carter-Reagan Presidential Debate, October 28, 1980. http://www.debates.org/index.php?page=october-28-1980-debate-transcript
[71] Casey Mulligan, "The Massive Tax Increase Hidden Inside Obamacare," Real Clear Markets, June 20, 2014. http://www.realclearmarkets.com/articles/2014/06/20/the_massive_tax_increase_hidden_inside_obamacare_101133.html
[72] Ibid.

On the Dark Side of the Laffer Curve
Capital Gains Tax

A decrease in the surtaxes to a more reasonable amount would result not only in a more economically sound structure, but would ultimately yield more in revenue to the government out of lower taxes than the government receives out of the higher taxes.[73]
— Warren G. Harding, *"Annual Report of the Secretary of the Treasury,"* 1923

Capital Gains Tax Revenues as a Share of GDP vs. Nominal and Real* Capital Gains Tax Rates
(annual, Rates: 1960-2016; Revenues: 1960-2013)

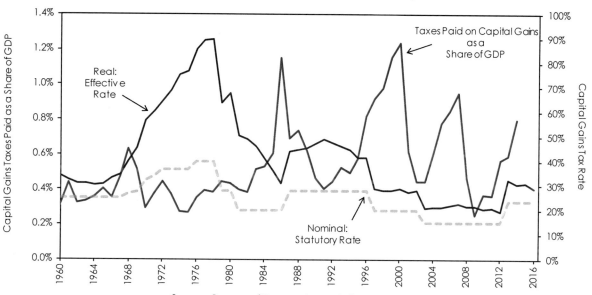

Source: Bureau of Economic Analysis, Bureau of Labor Statistics, Office of Tax Analysis

The tax on capital gains has always been and remains today a tax on nominal realized capital gains, i.e. the dollar difference between what an asset sold for and the dollar price paid for that asset no matter how many years the asset was held. To some extent, the tax paid is voluntary because people can choose when to buy and sell assets. Thus, if all prices are rising (inflation), the dollar price of an asset will rise simply because of generalized inflation. Therefore, by taxing nominal capital gains, illusory capital gains are taxed even when there has been no real appreciation. The real effective tax rate on capital gains illustrated above takes into account how inflation affects taxes (note the enormous surge in the real effective tax rate on capital gains in the 1970s as shown by the red line in the chart above).

This chart shows the relationship between the effective tax rate on real capital gains fully adjusted for inflation, the statutory tax rate and total capital gains tax receipts relative to GDP. Under inflationary conditions, the effective tax rate can be significantly higher than the statutory tax rate.

---

[73] Bruce Barlett, "Laffer Curve Part 3," October 1, 2012. http://papers.ssrn.com/sol3/papers.cfm?abstract_id=2155979

On careful examination, increases in capital gains tax rates are generally associated with lower capital gains tax revenues and lowered capital gains tax rates are associated with higher tax revenues. Here again is a tax on the wrong side of the Laffer Curve.

> *Investors' elasticity to capital gains rate changes may exceed unity, thus allowing rate cuts without impairing Treasury revenues.*[74]
> —*Harley Hinrichs, 1963*

---

[74] Bruce Bartlett, "Supply-Side Economics: 'Voodoo Economics' or Lasting Contribution?" Laffer Associates, November 11, 2003.

It Ain't Rocket Surgery—Larry Gatlin, 2015
Corporate Income Tax
High Marginal Tax Rates Discourage Investment, Yet Produce Little Revenue[75]

The 13% is a tax on business. Since 1950 business has reduced its contribution to the federal tax collection from 50% down to 20%. Individuals in the form of social security tax and individual income tax are paying 80%. I want to bring that back to where it was.
— Gov. Jerry Brown, March 13, 1992

Country	Corporate Income Tax Rate (%, 2016)
United States	38.92
France	34.43
Belgium	33.99
Italy	31.29
Germany	30.18
Australia	30.00
Japan	29.97
Luxembourg	29.22
Greece	29.00
New Zealand	28.00
Canada	26.70
Austria	25.00
Israel	25.00
Netherlands	25.00
Norway	25.00
Spain	25.00
Korea	24.20
Denmark	22.00
Sweden	22.00
Switzerland	21.15
Estonia	20.00
Finland	20.00
Iceland	20.00
Turkey	20.00
United Kingdom	20.00
Czech Republic	19.00
Slovenia	17.00
Ireland	12.50

Country	Corporate Income Tax Revenues % GDP (2013)
Norway	8.8
Australia	4.9
Luxembourg	4.8
New Zealand	4.4
Japan	4.0
Czech Republic	3.4
Korea	3.4
Israel	3.2
Italy	3.2
Belgium	3.1
Canada	3.0
Switzerland	2.8
Denmark	2.7
Sweden	2.6
France	2.5
Finland	2.4
Ireland	2.4
United Kingdom	2.4
Austria	2.2
Iceland	2.2
Spain	2.0
Netherlands	1.9
Turkey	1.9
United States	1.9
Germany	1.8
Greece	1.3
Slovenia	1.2
Estonia	0.3

[75] The table shows the U.S. vs. International: Highest Statutory Combined Corporate Income Tax Rate (Federal, State and Local) and Corporate Income Tax Revenue (again Federal, State and Local) as a Share of GDP. Note: We chose to examine countries that are members of the OECD. We were not able to display results for OECD member countries Chile, Hungary, Mexico, Poland, Portugal, Latvia and the Slovak Republic due to the OECD missing Corporate Income Tax Revenue data for these countries.

The U.S. has the highest corporate income tax rate in the OECD and the fifth lowest tax revenues. Germany has the fifth highest tax rate and fourth lowest tax revenues. The Czech Republic has the third lowest tax rate and the sixth highest tax revenues. This is the Laffer Curve in action. Slovenia and Estonia have low tax rates and low revenues. This too is the Laffer Curve in action. And then there's always Greece…

For nature is simple and does not indulge in the luxury of superfluous causes.
— Sir Isaac Newton, Principia, 1687

People Pay Taxes, Corporations Don't

Get rid of the loopholes. Level the playing field. And use the savings to lower the corporate tax rate for the first time in 25 years — without adding to our deficit. It can be done.[76]
— *President Barack Obama, 2011 State of the Union*

U.S. Corporate Income Tax Revenue as a % of GDP vs. U.S. Top Marginal Corporate Income Tax Rate
(annual, Tax Revenue and U.S. Marginal Rate: 1947 to 2015, OECD Rate: 1983-2015)

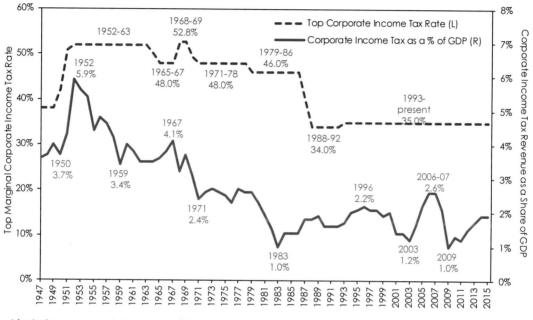

* includes average state and local tax rates

Source: IRS, OMB

The above chart shows the highest U.S. corporate tax rate back to 1947 on through 2015 and the corresponding corporate tax revenues as a share of GDP. From the late 1940s to the early 1950s, the corporate tax rate was raised significantly. Revenues rose at first and then declined precipitously as tax rates remained high. Companies adjusted to the higher tax rates and minimized tax liabilities.

A careful look at the chart shows how tax rate increases reduce revenues and tax rate reductions raise revenues. The Laffer Curve strikes once again.

I would like to replace all that [tax laws] with a flat, fair, honest tax of 13% on gross income and 13% on value added and bring in the exact same amount of revenue as you would get from the Social Security tax, the income tax, the corporate tax, the gift and estate, the gasoline tax, and I want to abolish all of those.[77]
— *Gov. Jerry Brown, 1992*

---

[76] "Remarks by the President in State of Union Address," January 25, 2011.
https://www.whitehouse.gov/the-press-office/2011/01/25/remarks-president-state-union-address
[77] Gov. Jerry Brown, 1992 Presidential Election, Democratic Candidates Debate, February 23, 1992.

High Corporate Tax Rates Make the U.S. Uncompetitive
Inversions: How the U.S. Lost its Tax Advantage

We should start with our tax code. Right now, companies get tax breaks for moving jobs and profits overseas. Meanwhile, companies that choose to stay in America get hit with one of the highest tax rates in the world. It makes no sense, and everyone knows it. So let's change it.[78]

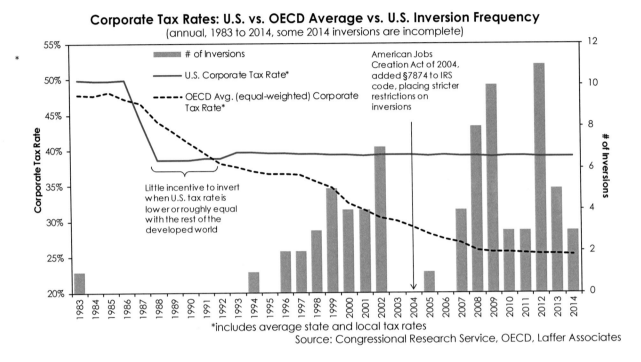

Corporate Tax Rates: U.S. vs. OECD Average vs. U.S. Inversion Frequency
(annual, 1983 to 2014, some 2014 inversions are incomplete)

*includes average state and local tax rates
Source: Congressional Research Service, OECD, Laffer Associates

The above chart shows the annual number of corporate inversions. An inversion is when a corporation moves corporate income to a foreign country with lower corporate tax rates. The lack of U.S. corporate tax competitiveness incentivizes corporations to seek inversions. Who says supply-side economics doesn't work? Not corporate boards or management!

In 1983 there was only one inversion when the U.S. corporate income tax rate was slightly higher than the OECD average. From 1984 through 1993 there were no inversions. From 1996 on, corporate inversions were commonplace. In 1987, the U.S. federal corporate income tax rate was reduced from 46% to 34%, which set into motion a worldwide movement to reduce corporate tax rates everywhere. Once the 1987 corporate tax rate cut was in place, the U.S. stopped reducing the corporate tax rate and foreign governments moved at an accelerated pace to reduce their corporate tax rates. In fact, the U.S., against all logic, actually increased the corporate income tax rate to 35% in 1993.

---

[78] "Remarks by the President in State of Union Address," January 24, 2012.
https://www.whitehouse.gov/the-press-office/2012/01/24/remarks-president-state-union-address

The previous page chart shows a statutory corporate tax rate (inclusive of state and local corporate tax rates as well) and also the dynamic average corporate tax rate for the OECD countries. By not cutting the corporate tax rate, the U.S. lost its competitive advantage and ended up in 2016 having the very highest corporate tax rate in the OECD.

The U.S. continues to lag behind the OECD with the highest statutory corporate tax rate in the developed world. Using a dynamic scoring model that takes into account reactions to policy changes, the Tax Foundation found the following:

> *The model estimates that cutting the federal corporate tax rate from 35% to 25% would raise GDP by 2.2%, increase the private-business capital stock by 6.2%, boost wages and hours of work by 1.9% and 0.3%, respectively, and increase total federal revenues by 0.8%.*[79]

[79] Michael Schuyler, "Growth Dividend from a Lower Corporate Tax Rate," The Tax Foundation, March 12, 2013. http://taxfoundation.org/article/growth-dividend-lower-corporate-tax-rate

Section V – Government Policy Actions: Regulations and Debt

George McGovern, the 1972 Democratic Party presidential nominee and his era's Bernie Sanders, Wedgwood Benn, or Teddy Kennedy, wrote the following in his article, "A Politician's Dream is a Businessman's Nightmare," The Wall Street Journal in 1992:[80]

In retrospect, I wish I had known more about the hazards and difficulties of such a business, especially during a recession of the kind that hit New England just as I was acquiring the inn's 43-year leasehold. I also wish that during the years I was in public office, I had had this firsthand experience about the difficulties business people face every day. That knowledge would have made me a better U.S. senator and a more understanding presidential contender.

Today we are much closer to a general acknowledgment that government must encourage business to expand and grow. Bill Clinton, Paul Tsongas, Bob Kerrey and others have, I believe, changed the debate of our party. We intuitively know that to create job opportunities we need entrepreneurs who will risk their capital against an expected payoff. Too often, however, public policy does not consider whether we are choking off those opportunities.

While I never have doubted the worthiness of any of these goals, the concept that most often eludes legislators is: "Can we make consumers pay the higher prices for the increased operating costs that accompany public regulation and government reporting requirements with reams of red tape." It is a simple concern that is nonetheless often ignored by legislators.

---

[80] George McGovern, "A Politician's Dream Is a Businessman's Nightmare: A 1992 column on the realities of running a business," Wall Street Journal, October 21, 2012. http://www.wsj.com/articles/SB10001424052 9702034064045780705435450227704

In short, "one-size-fits-all" rules for business ignore the reality of the marketplace. And setting thresholds for regulatory guidelines at artificial levels -- e.g., 50 employees or more, $500,000 in sales -- takes no account of other realities, such as profit margins, labor intensive vs. capital intensive businesses, and local market economics.

The problem we face as legislators is: Where do we set the bar so that it is not too high to clear? I don't have the answer. I do know that we need to start raising these questions more often.

When I took office, I inherited a heavy load of serious economic problems besides energy, and we've met them all head-on. We've slashed Government regulations and put free enterprise back into the airlines, the trucking and the financial systems of our country, and we're now doing the same thing for the railroads. This is the greatest change in the relationship between Government and business since the New Deal.
— President Jimmy Carter, Democratic Nomination Acceptance Speech, 1980

Gas Line under Jimmy Carter 1980 National Energy Plan

Source: Associated Press

It was at the time the gas lines were at their worst that the incredibly humorous Nixon/Ford economist Herb Stein said that he would prove mathematically that the length of a gas line could never exceed the length it took to drive through with one full tank of gas.

If you put the federal government in charge of the Sahara Desert, in five years there'd be a shortage of sand.
— Milton Friedman

According to John Childs[81], You Don't Get All the Government You Pay For (Thank Goodness)

The whole business thing is predicated a lot on the tax laws…It's why we rehearse in Canada and not in the U.S. A lot of our astute moves have been basically keeping up with tax laws, where to go, where not to put it. Whether to sit on it or not. We left England because we'd be paying 98 cents on the dollar. We left, and they lost out. No taxes at all.[82]
— Keith Richards, "Inside the Rolling Stones," 2002

To pay taxes, the costs taxpayers actually incur are far greater than the net sums the government collects.[83] Individuals and businesses as taxpayers must pay substantially more than $1 in order for government beneficiaries to receive $1 of federal government services. Before individuals and businesses pay their tax liability, they must first spend time collecting records, organizing files, and wading through the tax code to determine exactly what their tax liability is. In addition, individuals purchase products and services, such as tax software or an accountant, to assist them in determining their tax liability. These are tax compliance outlays. Thirdly, in effect, taxpayers must also pay the administrative costs needed to run the IRS etc., solely for tax collection purposes. Still there is more.

Businesses, large and small, hire teams of accountants, lawyers, and tax professionals to track, measure, and pay their taxes. This tax infrastructure is also used to optimize the tax liability of the business. Individuals and businesses change their behavior in response to tax policies, hiring tax experts to discover ways to minimize their tax liabilities. The efficiency costs from both legal tax avoidance and illegal tax evasion are difficult to quantify, but could be the highest costs of all.

One can only imagine what the full burden of government on the well-being of society might be. In our analysis we estimate that U.S. taxpayers pay $431.1 billion annually, or 30 percent of total income taxes collected, just to comply with and administer the U.S. income tax system.[84] This cost estimate includes:

- Approximately $31.5 billion in direct outlays (e.g. paying a professional tax preparer such as H&R Block or purchasing tax software) (2010 data).

---

81 Our dear friend John Childs is the CEO and founder of J.W. Childs Associates, a private equity firm based in Boston. He also worked for Thomas H. Lee Partners where he was instrumental in the purchase of Snapple.
82 Andy Serwer, "Inside the Rolling Stones Inc.," Fortune, September 30, 2002. http://www.wsj.com/articles/SB10001424127887324634304578535670594929286
83 For more on this topic, see: Arthur B. Laffer, Wayne H. Winegarden and John Childs, "The Economic Burden Caused by Tax Code Complexity," The Laffer Center for Supply-Side Economics, April 2011.
84 According to the IRS, total gross individual income tax collections in 2008 were $1.4 trillion (http://www.irs.gov/pub/irs-soi/08db01co.xls); Although as of this writing total tax collections from 2010 are available, the detailed breakdown of income taxes paid by adjusted gross income are only available through 2008. For consistency, data on tax collections from 2008 are used throughout this study.

- Total IRS administrative costs of $12.4 billion (2010 data).

- The Taxpayer Advocacy Service of the IRS estimates that individuals and businesses also spent 6.1 billion hours complying with the filing requirements of the U.S. income tax code. We estimate the dollar value or cost of these hours to be $377.9 billion as of 2008. The 6.1 billion hours number was estimated by multiplying the number of copies of each form filed in tax year 2008 by the average amount of time the IRS estimated it took to complete the form.

  o Individuals spent 3.16 billion hours complying with the income tax code, which weighted by time spent by income group, costs the U.S. economy $216.2 billion annually.

  o Businesses spent $2.94 billion complying with the business income tax code, which cost the U.S. economy $161.7 billion.

  o Comprehensive audits also impose an additional taxpayer burden of at least $9.3 billion annually.

That's the whole point of the flat tax, everyone can fill it out on a postcard. You find out what you earned, deduct rent and charity or your home mortgage, and you multiply by 13. It's simple, it's clean, and it cuts out all the corruption in Washington, which raises money by selling loopholes, none of which are for us.[85]
— Gov. Jerry Brown, 1992

[85] Gov. Jerry Brown, 1992 Presidential Election, Democratic Candidates Debate, March 15, 1992.

Excessive Regulations

We have to make America the best place on Earth to do business. We need to take responsibility for our deficit and reform our government. That's how our people will prosper. That's how we'll win the future.[86]
— *President Barack Obama, 2011 State of the Union*

There you go again.
— *Ronald Reagan's retort to President Jimmy Carter's proposal to expand government in their 1980 debate*

Do not imagine, comrades, that leadership is a pleasure. On the contrary, it is a deep and heavy responsibility. No one believes more firmly than Comrade Napoleon that all animals are equal. He would be only too happy to let you make your decisions yourselves. But sometimes you might make wrong decisions, comrades, and then where should we be?
— *Squealer, from Animal Farm*

Pages in the CCH Standard Federal Tax Reporter vs. Annual Pages in the Federal Register[87]
(annual, 1950-2014)

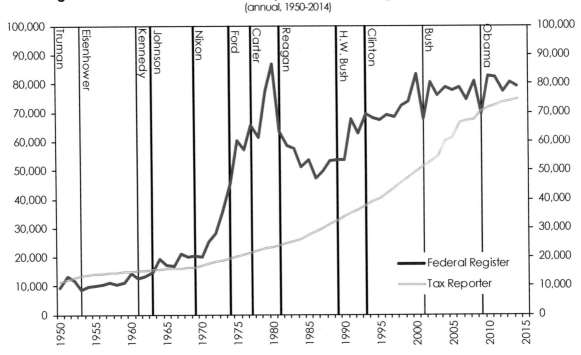

Source: CCH, Office of the Federal Register

---

[86] "Remarks by the President in State of Union Address," January 25, 2011.
https://www.whitehouse.gov/the-press-office/2011/01/25/remarks-president-state-union-address
[87] The Federal Register is a publication that records new regulations that become law in a given year. If, for example the Federal Register is 80,000 pages in one year and 70,000 pages in the next year, this reduction of 10,000 pages doesn't represent a repeal of 10,000 pages of regulations, but rather shows a slowing in the rate of addition of pages of regulation.

Tax Complexity is a Tax on Paying Taxes—Dan Mitchell

Estimated Hourly Costs of IRS Paperwork 2016[88]

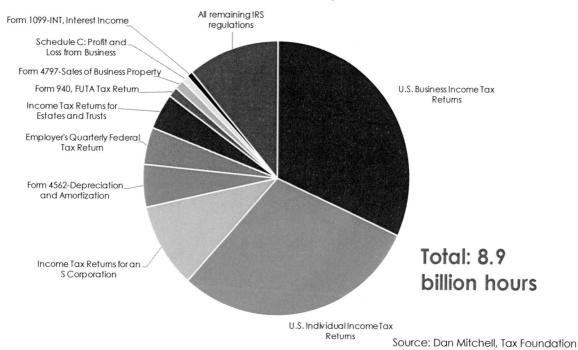

Form 1099-INT, Interest Income
Schedule C: Profit and Loss from Business
Form 4797-Sales of Business Property
Form 940, FUTA Tax Return
Income Tax Returns for Estates and Trusts
Employer's Quarterly Federal Tax Return
Form 4562-Depreciation and Amortization
Income Tax Returns for an S Corporation
All remaining IRS regulations
U.S. Business Income Tax Returns
U.S. Individual Income Tax Returns

Total: 8.9 billion hours

Source: Dan Mitchell, Tax Foundation

Estimated Compliance Costs of IRS Paperwork 2016

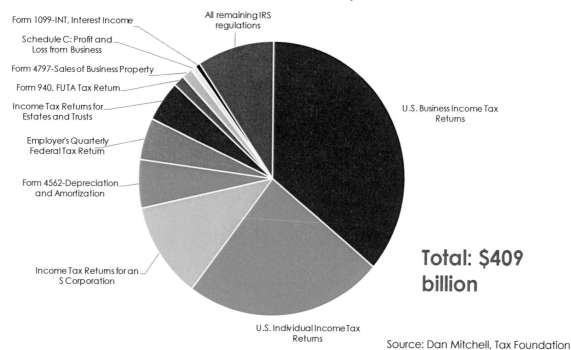

Form 1099-INT, Interest Income
Schedule C: Profit and Loss from Business
Form 4797-Sales of Business Property
Form 940, FUTA Tax Return
Income Tax Returns for Estates and Trusts
Employer's Quarterly Federal Tax Return
Form 4562-Depreciation and Amortization
Income Tax Returns for an S Corporation
All remaining IRS regulations
U.S. Business Income Tax Returns
U.S. Individual Income Tax Returns

Total: $409 billion

Source: Dan Mitchell, Tax Foundation

---

[88] Dan Mitchell, "Tax Complexity is a Tax on Paying Taxes," International Liberty Blog, July 20, 2016.
https://danieljmitchell.wordpress.com/2016/07/20/tax-complexity-is-a-tax-on-paying-taxes/

Section VI – Government Policy Actions: Tariffs, Quotas, Capital Controls and Other Trade Barriers

The benefits of trade accrue to everyone; importers, exporters, consumers and producers of all trading nations. The consumption of foreign-made, more economically produced products makes everyone—consumers and producers—better off. And each and every impediment to trade irrespective of which country imposes the impediment hurts both the exporting country and the importing country. The benefits of trade are best measured as total trade—exports plus imports.

Politicians believe trade to be a "zero-sum game." By "zero-sum" we mean exports create jobs and imports displace jobs. Using jobs as our measure of good and bad, what's good for us (exports) is bad for foreigners and vice versa. In other words, if we're better off, they're worse off.

Trade is not about jobs at all or even about total employment. Instead, trade is about the value of income.

Ignorance of the benefits of trade is probably the only product that is freely traded without borders. Governments far and wide believe that imposing unanswered protectionist measures advantages their economy at the expense of their trading partners' economies (the concept of a zero-sum game). For politicians who insist that trade and trade protectionist measures are all about jobs, their measure of success would be the trade balance—exports minus imports.

Advocates of protectionist measures make at least two serious mistakes. First, they ignore the benefits to the importing country from the consumption of imports. And, second, they fabricate illusionary increases in employment by assuming reduced imports are not offset by reduced exports.

Each country exports some of the products it produces to earn the wherewithal to pay for imports from other countries. This relationship between exports and imports among countries is no different than the relationship between income and spending amongst individuals. Income is earned by producing goods, which are sold in order to buy goods others produce. A country's imports equal its exports without capital flows.

Lerner's symmetry theorem—which is math, not ideology—simply states that there is a precise correspondence between taxes on imports (tariffs) and taxes on exports. Both taxes on imports or exports have the same effect on jobs (none) and on the gains from trade—hugely negative.

With regards to capital flows, we would ask which is preferable: capital trying to get into a country, or capital trying to get out of a country?

Politicians universally frame their country's trade deficit as costing jobs. But, in the same breath, they love net capital inflows. Politicians argue that capital inflows create jobs. Capital inflows provide the wherewithal to employ domestic workers.

In truth, the only way a country can have capital inflows is if it buys more goods from foreigners and sells less goods to foreigners, i.e. it has a trade deficit. The trade deficit is one and the same as the capital surplus. That's accounting (and economics). Any and all trade barriers hurt capital flows, exports and imports. Everyone is worse off. And any attempt to retaliate against foreign protectionism only makes all matters worse.

Protectionism Doesn't Bring Jobs Back[89]

As tragic as the marginal farmer's plight might be, no GOP argument, political or economic, could justify higher tariffs. By restricting foreigners' ability to sell their goods in the U.S., the Republicans were making it more difficult for foreigners to pay off their debts to the U.S. and import goods from us. Over time, tariffs would, in essence, have the same inhibiting impact on investment and commerce as an increase in taxes. Herbert Hoover signed the Smoot-Hawley Bill on June 16, 1930, but the stock market started anticipating the act as early as December 1928.
— *Jude Wanniski, Wall Street Journal, 1977*

Tariffs and Total Trade Surrounding the 1930 Smoot-Hawley Tariff
(Trade: annual, $ bil., 1925 to 1939, Dow Jones: monthly, Jan-25 to Dec-39, end-of-period)

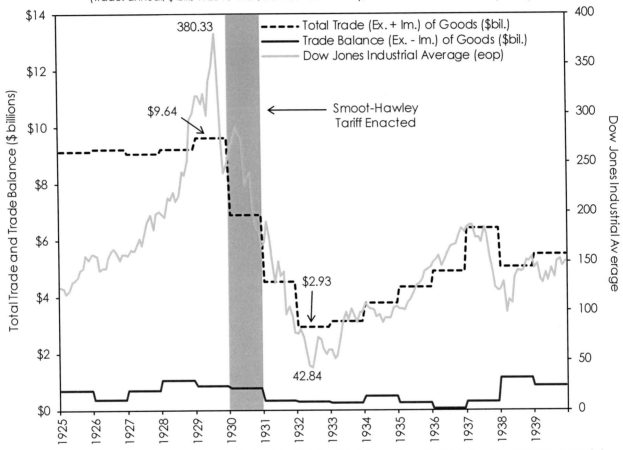

Source: Bureau of Economic Analysis, Historical Statistics of the U.S., U.S. International Trade Commission

In the late 1920s, a major piece of protectionist legislation was passed by the full House and Senate in 1929. It was signed into law by President Herbert Hoover in June of 1930. The chart above illustrates the devastating effect those tariffs had on total trade (exports plus imports), the stock market and unemployment. This is the story of the catastrophic Smoot-Hawley Tariff legislation that led to the demise of President Hoover's Administration and the U.S. economy. Thus, began the Great Depression.

---

[89] NOTE: the increase in the blue line attributable to the Smoot-Hawley tariff doesn't fully capture just how large the tariff was because it doesn't account for all of the adjustments made in the economy as a result of the tariff.

The lesson is that trade protection measures destroy the gains from trade by lowering total trade (exports plus imports), but create no jobs, as shown by the trade balance (exports minus imports). As it was in the past, so will it be in the future.

It is true that the tariff was reduced, so that the articles that were imported paid only about half as much in proportion after the change as before. But then the new laws increased the importations so much, that the loss was very much more than made up to the treasury, and the emperor found in a very short time that the state of his finances was greatly improved.[90]
— Peter the Great, 1690

Ancient Jerusalem Wall built to keep people out.

---

[90] Jacob Abbott, Peter the Great, p. 82, 1900.

Taxes Caused the Great Depression

The Smoot Hawley tariff was the largest peacetime increase in U.S. taxes on traded products ever (see previous page) and it was the catalyst for the Great Depression. Massive retaliation by foreign governments quickly followed. Huge federal and state tax increases in 1932 doubled down on the initial decline in the economy. And then, additional large tax increases in 1936 were the proximate cause of the economy's further relapse in 1937.

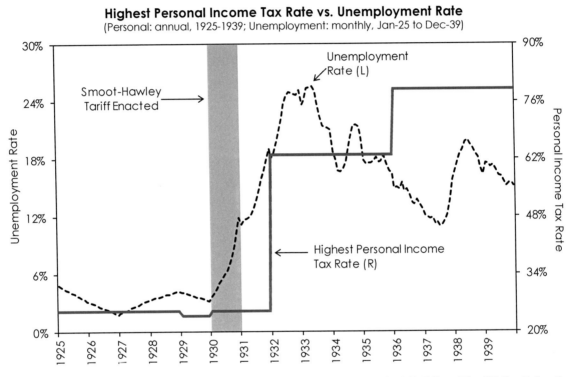

Highest Personal Income Tax Rate vs. Unemployment Rate
(Personal: annual, 1925-1939; Unemployment: monthly, Jan-25 to Dec-39)

Source: Bureau of Labor Statistics, Historical Statistics of the U.S, Tax Policy Center

On January 1st, 1932 the lowest personal income tax rate was raised from less than one half of one percent to 4% and the highest tax rate was raised from 25% to 63%. The corporate tax rate was raised from 12% to 13.75%. The highest inheritance tax rate was raised from 20% to 45%, and the gift tax was reinstituted at 33.5%. In 1929 state and local taxes were 7.2% of GDP and then rose to 8.5%, 9.7% and 12.3% for the years 1930, '31 and '32 respectively.

The economy got a lot worse, and President Hoover was resoundingly defeated in November 1932 by President Roosevelt.

In early 1933 the federal government declared a bank holiday, prohibiting banks from paying out gold or dealing in foreign exchange. An executive order made it illegal for anyone to "hoard" gold and forced everyone to turn in their gold and gold certificates to the government at an exchange value of $20.67 per ounce of gold in return for paper currency and bank deposits. All gold clauses in contracts private and public were declared null and void. By the end of January 1934 the price of gold, most of which had been confiscated, was raised by the government to $35 per ounce. In less than a year, the government confiscated as much gold as it could at $20.67 an ounce and then devalued the dollar in terms of gold by almost 60%. The confiscation cost gold holders in forgone gains over $6 billion in 1933 dollars when nominal GNP was $57.5 billion. That's one helluva tax.

Stock ticker manufactured by Edison and Unger, circa 1890.

In 1934 the highest estate tax rate was again raised from 45% to 60% and then to 70% in 1935. The highest gift tax rate went from 33.5% in 1933 to 45% in 1934 and 52.5% in 1935. The highest corporate tax rate was raised to 15% in 1936 and in 1937 a surtax on undistributed profits up to 27% was enacted. Finally, in 1936 the highest personal income tax rate was raised to 79%. The payroll tax rate was introduced at a rate of 1% of payroll in 1936, before increasing to 2% in 1937, and 3% in 1938. Doesn't all of this sound depressing both literally and figuratively?

The Truth About Tax Revenues

At this stage in the Template we, like Archilochus' fox, have inspected tax rates, tax bases and tax revenues from many perspectives. The big question is just what do the various tax policies do to provide our country's federal government with the necessary wherewithal to fund public services? While it's obvious that if all tax rates were zero, no matter how large the tax bases, there wouldn't be any tax revenues. Likewise, if all tax rates were in excess of 100%, there wouldn't be any tax base to tax and tax revenues would also be non-existent. In the real world however tax rates generally aren't zero nor are they over 100%. So based on the past 70 years of data, what should tax rates be to <u>best</u> provide the requisite tax revenues at the least damage to the private sector?

In order to bypass spurious correlation arising from population growth, inflation and trend growth in output per adult, we have plotted i.) Real Federal Tax Receipts per Adult Detrended against ii.) Real GDP per Adult Detrended, quarterly from the first quarter of 1950 to the third quarter of 2016 in the chart below. This chart shows visually the sensitivity of tax revenues to the tax base. Relationships just don't get any better.

Real GDP Per Adult and Real Federal Receipts Deviations from Trend
(quarterly, 1Q-50 to 4Q-16)

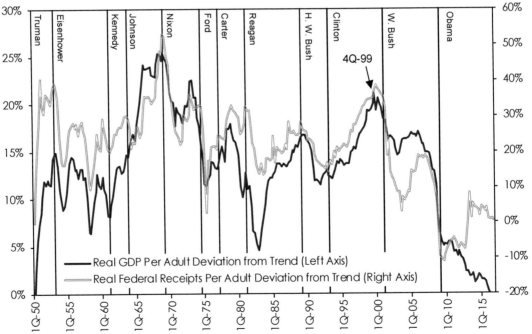

Source: Bureau of Economic Analysis, Bureau of Labor Statistics, Laffer Associates

Tax rates have two effects on tax revenues: First "the arithmetic effect" is the effect that when tax rates change, tax revenues per dollar of tax base change in the same direction and by the

Diogenes with his lantern trying to find an honest man.

same percentage as the tax rate change itself. And secondly, the "the economic effect" shows that when tax rates change the tax base also changes but in the opposite direction from the tax rate change. The "economic effect" thus always works in the opposite direction from the "arithmetic effect". It would appear from the chart above that in this age old struggle the tax base, or "economic effect", is the winner. At least it is in the U.S. over the past 70 years.

Federal tax revenue surges are the byproduct of exceptional economic performance and Federal tax revenue shortfalls go hand in hand with economic stagnation. Exceptional economic performance in turn is a consequence of tax rate cuts and stagnation is the bastard child of tax rate hikes. No better examples of the two extremes exist than the success of the U.S. economy and budget under President Bill Clinton and the failure of the U.S. economy and budget under President Barack Obama. Economics is all about incentives and is not Republican or Democrat, left-wing or right-wing, liberal or conservative. It's economics.

"Rich" Countries Awash in Debt

Raising America's debt limit...is a sign that the U.S. government can't pay its own bills. Increasing America's debt weakens us domestically and internationally...Washington is shifting the burden of bad choices today onto the backs of our children and grandchildren. America has a debt problem and a failure of leadership...I therefore intend to oppose the effort to increase America's debt limit.[91]
— *Then-Senator Barack Obama, Speech in the Senate, 2006*

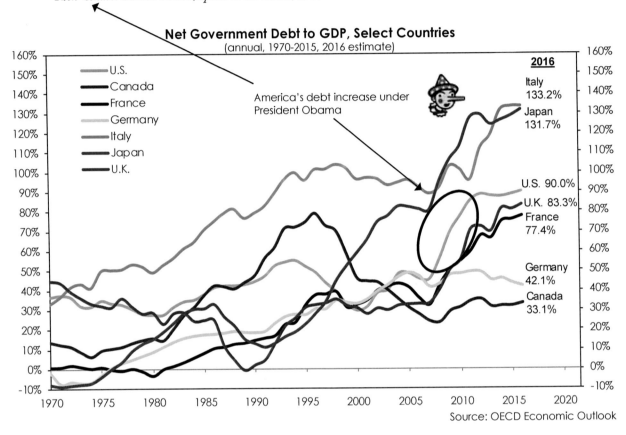

Net Government Debt to GDP, Select Countries
(annual, 1970-2015, 2016 estimate)

Legend:
- U.S.
- Canada
- France
- Germany
- Italy
- Japan
- U.K.

America's debt increase under President Obama

2016

Italy 133.2%
Japan 131.7%
U.S. 90.0%
U.K. 83.3%
France 77.4%
Germany 42.1%
Canada 33.1%

Source: OECD Economic Outlook

For you who worry about debt (We're with you), this chart shows net federal debt to GDP for a handful of countries. These figures do <u>not</u> include state and local debt <u>nor</u> do they include unfunded liabilities of government programs (such as Social Security, Medicare, etc. etc.). For you who don't worry, you must be on drugs.

Excessive debt raises the specter of increased taxes to fund interest payments and decreased

[91] "Increasing the Statutory Limit on the Public Debt," Congressional Record—Senate, March 16, 2006. https://www.gpo.gov/fdsys/pkg/CREC-2006-03-16/pdf/CREC-2006-03-16-pt1-PgS2236.pdf

confidence from a risk of default. High debt creates a vicious cycle of even greater debt as shown by the following table summarized from the previous chart:

Top Four Rankings of Net Government Debt to GDP

	2000	2005	2010	2016
1	Italy	Italy	Japan	Italy
2	Japan	Japan	Italy	Japan
3	Canada	Germany	U.S.	U.S.
4	Germany	U.S.	UK	UK

Within the budget, rising interest costs will crowd out programs that help ensure our future, including education, transportation and other physical infrastructure, research and development, and national security. Increased federal borrowing also crowds out private investments that promote growth in the economy. In addition, programs that protect the most vulnerable Americans could face sharp, sudden reductions if we don't have a sustainable fiscal outlook.[92]
— *Peter G. Peterson Foundation*

---

[92] "The Fiscal & Economic Challenge," Peter G. Peterson Foundation. http://www.pgpf.org/the-fiscal-and-economic-challenge

All In: It's Heads, I Win, Tails, You Lose[93]
Why Families Can't Get Ahead

...we have had 11 tax cuts since World War II and, in 10 out of those 11 cases, government revenues increased within a year. In the eleventh case—1948—it took two years for that to occur.[94]
— *Irving Kristol, 1979*

Federal and S&L Outlays, Federal Deficits, and Federal Regulatory Costs as a Share of GDP
(Federal Deficit, Regulatory Costs, Federal Outlays: 1990, 2000, 2010, 2015;
S&L Outlays: 1990, 2000, 2010, 2013)

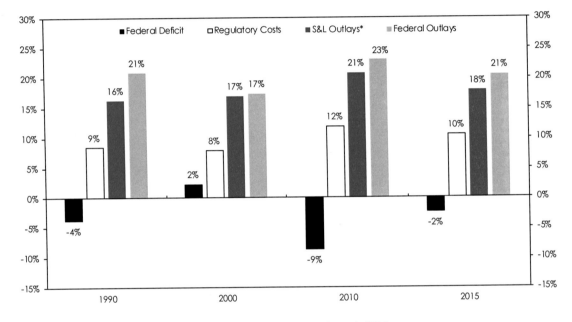

* The most recent S&L data release is 2013.

Source: Census Bureau, Competitive Enterprise Institute, Congressional Budget Office, Office of Management and Budget

With federal outlays the size they are and the size of state and local outlays plus the overwhelming size of regulatory costs, it's a wonder there's anything left over for America's families.

> *The doubters would have us turn back the clock with tax increases that would offset the personal tax-rate reductions already passed by this Congress. Raise present taxes to cut future deficits, they tell us. Well, I don't believe we should buy that argument...Higher taxes would not mean lower deficits. If they did, how would we explain that tax revenues more than doubled just since 1976; yet in that same 6-year period we ran the largest series of deficits in our history...Raising taxes won't balance the budget; it will encourage more government spending and less private investment.[95]*
> — *President Ronald Reagan, 1982 State of the Union*

---

[93] Ancient government prophecy.
[94] Irving Kristol, "Populist Remedy for Populist Abuses," in The Economics of the Tax Revolt, ed. Arthur B. Laffer & Jan P. Seymour, p. 52, 1979.
[95] Bruce Bartlett, "'Starve the Beast': Origins and Development of a Budgetary Metaphor," Laffer Associates, June 26, 2007.

Economics is Global
"Hooray for King Dollar"—Larry Kudlow

U.S. Dollar Index vs. Dow Jones Spot Commodity Index
(monthly, Jan-75 to Sep-16)

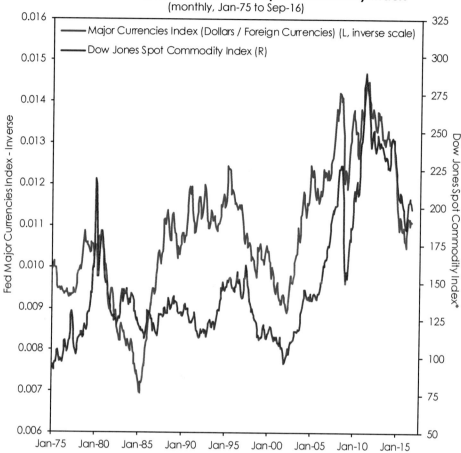

* Commodity index estimated by Laffer Associates since being discontinued by Dow Jones in April 2002
Source: Federal Reserve Board, Bloomberg

Commodities are global. Translating global supply and demand into dollars and cents requires an exchange rate where the dollar is one side of that exchange rate. The weaker the dollar, the higher commodity prices and the stronger the dollar, the lower are commodity prices. In terms of the domestic economy, a strong dollar usually means lower inflation and economic policies that are attractive to global capital. Both foreign and domestic capital will try to move into a country that has the right set of policies. In so doing, the country will have a capital surplus, a trade deficit, a strong currency and stable prices. If, for whatever reason, the country with the good set of economic policies tries to prevent its currency from appreciating, then its inflation rate will rise. Such is exactly what we describe in the case of England (pages 106-108) and Ireland (page 109).

The truth is hiding in plain sight.

The U.S. $, Capital Surplus, Economic Growth, Inflation and Tax Rates

Real GDP Growth, Trade Balance, U.S. Dollar Strength Index, U.S. Inflation Rate
(2nd Half of 1978 through 1st Half of 1985, real GDP growth is semiannual SAAR, trade balance is % of GDP, U.S. dollar strength is as measured by the Fed's real trade-weighted major currency index, inflation rate is YoY % change)

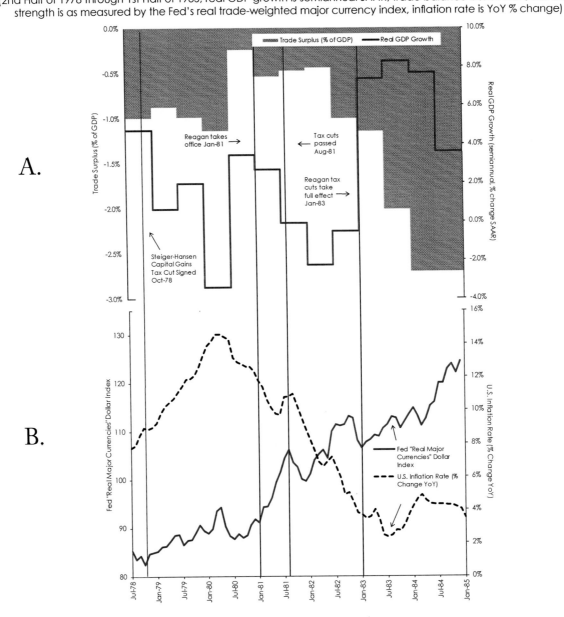

The principles illustrated in these charts are i.) Sidney Alexander's Absorption Principle and ii.) Léon Walras' Law of One Price.

When supply-side pro-growth policies (especially tax rate reductions) are adopted in one country, that pro-growth country's after-tax rates of return for both investments and labor will increase relative to the rest of the world. Foreign as well as domestic investors try to augment their holdings of assets in the now-more-attractive country. Stock prices and employment will rise.

For domestic investors, asset values and investment rates will rise. For foreign investors, capital will move to the now-more-attractive country. Imports into the more attractive country will rise while exports from the more attractive country will fall or, there must be an increase in the now-more-attractive country's capital surplus and a larger trade deficit, Alexander's absorption principle (see chart A).

But increasing exports to and reducing imports from the more attractive country requires an increase in the more attractive country's terms-of-trade, which is one and the same as a reduction in that country's competitiveness. Making the more attractive country's goods less competitive requires either an exchange rate appreciation or domestic inflation or some combination of each: the Law of One Price as shown on the previous page "Economics is Global."

As shown in chart B, the U.S. did it just right under President Reagan. The dollar rose a lot, domestic inflation fell, the U.S. trade deficit expanded enormously and U.S. real GDP growth rose to all-time highs—all because of supply-side economic policies.

Other countries didn't do quite as well with their economic policies as the U.S. did, and they paid a dear political price for their errors.

Walras' law of one price implies that exchange rate changes will mirror inflation differences i.e. during the same time period countries with stronger currencies will have less inflation than countries with weaker currencies.

Alexander's absorption principle asserts that capital will flow to faster growth countries out of slower growth countries i.e. an increase in a country's growth rate will worsen that country's trade balance and increase its exchange rate or inflation rate.

Section VIII – Government Policy Actions: The Benefits from Trade

On page 80, we discuss the damaging effects of tariffs, quotas and non-tariff barriers. This section looks at why international trade is so important to the wellbeing of all countries.

i.) Autarky – a world without trade

Imagine only five people in the whole world, each of whom produces a given product, say, apples in Ohio, coffee in Costa Rica, kiwis in New Zealand, bananas in Africa, and silk in China. If there were no trade, each producer would consume only what that producer produces. The same consumption day in and day out would soon get pretty tiresome. Without trade, you'd have five unexcited, but fully employed, producers who have to consume what they alone produce.

ii.) The consumption gains from trade

Now, imagine trade. The apple producer trades some of his apples for bananas, coffee, kiwis, and silk, as do the producers of silk, coffee, kiwis, and bananas. Just how far this trade would go depends upon the preferences of each of the five producers. But everyone would be better off, <u>not because of more jobs</u>, but because <u>trade enhances the quality of income</u>. The monotony of consuming only one product is replaced by novel, new and more exciting products acquired through trade. This is called the "consumption gains from trade."

iii.) The production gains from trade

When the producers in various countries engage in trade, each country will produce and export products they produce relatively more efficiently and import products they produce relatively less efficiently. Total production everywhere will be higher, with the exact same amount of employment. These gains from relative differences in efficiency are called the "production gains from trade." This diversification of consumption and production is what trade is all about. It's called a win / win, the gains from trade, comparative advantage. It's the economics made famous by the English economist David Ricardo.

iv.) Protectionism hurts everyone everywhere

Any country's protectionism hurts each country's economy by reducing the quality of each country's consumption and production via total trade (exports plus imports). Retaliatory protectionist measures do not offset the damage done by the original protectionist policies, but instead, these retaliatory measures cause even greater overall damage to both economies.

To see this point, imagine the U.S. develops a cure for colon cancer and Japan develops a cure for Alzheimer's. Also, imagine Japan disallows the import of the U.S. cure for colon cancer to Japan. Should the U.S. prohibit Japan from selling its cure for Alzheimer's in the U.S.? NO! Japan's protectionism hurts Japanese consumers (they die from more colon cancer). Any retaliation with additional U.S. protectionist measures would devastate Americans with Alzheimer's.

v.) Export earnings pay for imports

To acquire the gains from trade, each country uses the products it produces (exports) to trade for the products other countries produce (imports). Exports earn the wherewithal to pay for imports. The relationship between exports and imports among countries is no different than the relationship between income and spending amongst individuals. Each country earns income by producing and exporting goods, the proceeds from which are used to buy goods other countries produce.

Boiling it all down, countries sell products to foreigners (exports) in order to buy products from foreigners (imports). And as such, any attempt to reduce imports is precisely equivalent to a measure to reduce exports—Lerner's Symmetry Theorem.

vi.) The international capital account is the converse of the trade amount

Another important point to realize is that the trade surplus or deficit is one and the same as the capital deficit or surplus.

Foreigners generate a dollar cash flow by selling more goods to U.S. and by buying less goods from U.S., which allows them to buy U.S.-located assets. The trade balance of a country in balance of payments accounting terms is the counter account to a country's capital balance. Thus, a country's trade surplus is also its capital deficit and its trade deficit is also its capital surplus. In order for the U.S. to have a net capital inflow, foreigners have to have a trade surplus with the U.S.

Imports and Exports

Trade in OECD Countries: Imports and Exports as a Share of GDP
(annual, 2014)

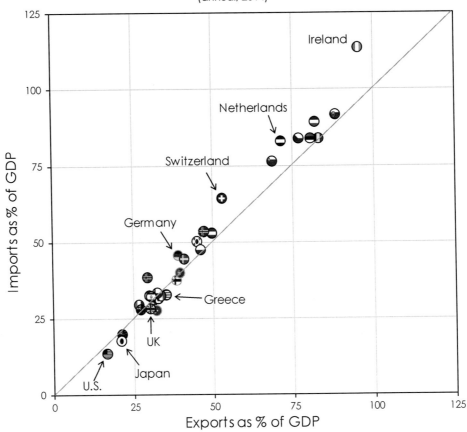

Note: Luxembourg is excluded.

Each country exports some of the products it produces to earn the wherewithal to pay for imports from other countries. This relationship between exports and imports among countries is no different than the relationship between income and spending amongst individuals. Income is earned by producing goods, which are sold in order to buy goods others produce. A country's imports equal its exports without capital flows. Countries other than those named included in the above chart are:

Australia	Austria	Belgium	Canada	Chile
Czech Republic	Denmark	Estonia	Finland	France
Hungary	Iceland	Israel	Italy	Korea
Mexico	New Zealand	Norway	Poland	Portugal
Slovakia	Slovenia	Spain	Sweden	Turkey

Even though economics is a very old subject, it has not truly come to grips with the main difficulty, which is the inordinate practical importance of a few extreme events.
— Mandelbrot, 1983

The Laffer Curve:
Voodoo Economics or Lasting Contribution? Part I

I have called this paper an analytical review of "supply-side economics", a term associated in the United States with extravagant claims about the effects of changes in the tax structure on capital accumulation. In a sense, the analysis I have reviewed supports these claims: Under what I view as conservative assumptions, I estimated that eliminating capital income taxation would increase capital stock by about 35 percent. Achieved over a ten year period, such an increase would more than double the annual growth rate of the U.S. capital stock… The supply-side economists, if that is the right term for those whose research I have been discussing, have delivered the largest genuinely free lunch I have seen in 25 years in this business, and I believe we would have a better society if we followed their advice.
—Bob Lucas, Nobel laureate in Economics, "Supply-Side Economics: An Analytical Review," 1990. [96]

History offers not a shred of support for faith in the pro-growth effects of tax cuts.
—Paul Krugman, Nobel laureate in Economics, writing in the New York Times, April 24, 2017. [97]

Americans, that is, residents of the United States, work much more than do Europeans. Using labor market statistics from the Organisation for Economic Co-operation and Development (OECD), I find that Americans on a per person aged 15–64 basis work in the market sector 50 percent more than do the French. This was not always the case. In the early 1970s, Americans allocated less time to the market than did the French. The comparisons between Americans and Germans or Italians are the same. Why are there such large differences in labor supply across these countries? Why did the relative labor supplies change so much over time? In this article, I determine the importance of tax rates in accounting for these differences in labor supply for the major advanced industrial countries and find that tax rates alone account for most of them.
—Edward C. Prescott, Nobel laureate in Economics, "Why Do Americans Work More than Europeans," 2003. [98]

Frankly, I think supply-side economics is snake oil.
—Robert Reich, former Secretary of Labor under Bill Clinton, comment on Dr. Laffer's The End of Prosperity, 2008.

Tax reduction is what I've been pushing for since the early 1970's. When income tax rates go above 25 percent, 'people find so many ways to get around them that the high rates become counterproductive.
—Robert A. Mundell, Nobel laureate in Economics, on the passage of the 1986 Tax Reform Act, 1986. [99]

An example of fad economics occurred in 1980, when a small group of economists advised presidential candidate Ronald Reagan that an across-the-board cut in income tax rates would raise tax revenue. They argued that if people could keep a higher fraction of their income, people would work harder to earn more income. Even though tax rates would be lower, income would rise by so much, they claimed, that tax revenue would rise. Almost all professional economists, including most of those who supported Reagan's proposal to cut taxes, viewed this outcome as far too optimistic. Lower tax rates might encourage people to work harder, and this extra effort would offset the direct effects of lower tax rates. George Bush, also a presidential candidate in 1980, agreed with most of the professional economists. He called this idea, "voodoo economics." Nonetheless, the argument was appealing to Reagan, and it shaped the 1980 presidential campaign and the economic policies of the 1980s.
—Greg Mankiw, Professor of Economics at Harvard, "Charlatans and Cranks, Principles of Microeconomics, Vol. 1, 1998.

It would seem that some economists prefer complex error over simple truth.

---

[96] Robert E. Lucas, Jr. "Supply-Side Economics: An Analytical Review," Oxford Economic Papers, New Series, Vol. 42. No. 2 (Apr. 1990). pp. 293-316. http://piketty.pse.ens.fr/files/Lucas2000.pdf
[97] https://www.nytimes.com/2017/04/24/opinion/zombies-of-voodoo-economics.html?_r=0
[98] https://www.minneapolisfed.org/research/qr/qr2811.pdf
[99] http://www.nytimes.com/1986/01/12/business/eccentric-economist-robert-a-mundell-supply-side-s-intellectual-guru.html?scp=1689&sq=economic+theory&st=nyt

The Laffer Curve:
Voodoo Economics or Lasting Contribution? Part II

Tax reduction thus sets off a process that can bring gains for everyone, gains won by marshalling resources that would otherwise stand idle—workers without jobs and farm and factory capacity without markets. Yet many taxpayers seemed prepared to deny the nation the fruits of tax reduction because they question the financial soundness of reducing taxes when the federal budget is already in deficit. Let me make clear why, in today's economy, fiscal prudence and responsibility call for tax reduction even if it temporarily enlarged the federal deficit—why reducing taxes is the best way open to us to increase revenues.
—President John F. Kennedy "Economic Report of the President", January 1963.

Greg Mankiw retitled his Charlatans and Cranks section after complaints from an editor and some readers that the title was "too inflammatory for a textbook description of a policy debate."[100] Starting with the 2nd edition of his textbook published in the year 2000, the section was retitled "The Laffer Curve and Supply-side Economics." He had this to say to about the Laffer Curve in 2010:

My guess is that that the short-run answer and the long-run answer are quite different. For example, if you raised the top rate from 35 to, say, 60 percent, you might raise revenue in the short run. Over time, however, you would get lower economic growth, so the additional revenues would fall off and eventually decline below what they would have been at the lower rate.... I will pass on offering a specific number, as it would require more time and thought than I can offer just now, but I will opine that I think the long-run answer is actually more important for policy purposes than the short-run answer.
—Greg Mankiw, Professor of Economics at Harvard, when asked "Where does the Laffer Curve Bend?" the Washington Post, 2010.[101]

Why look for the rate that maximizes revenue? As the tax rate rises, the "deadweight loss" (real loss to the economy rises) so as the rate gets close to maximizing revenue the loss to the economy exceeds the gain in revenue.... I dislike budget deficits as much as anyone else. But would I really want to give up say $1 billion of GDP in order to reduce the deficit by $100 million? No. National income is a goal in itself. That is what drives consumption and our standard of living.
—Martin Feldstein, Professor of Economics at Harvard, when asked "Where does the Laffer Curve Bend?" the Washington Post, 2010.[102]

To the extent that a tax cut succeeds in stimulating business, our progressive tax system will collect extra revenues out of the higher income levels. Hence a tax cut may in the long run imply little (or even no) loss in federal revenues, and hence no substantial increase in the long run public debt.
—Paul Samuelson, Nobel laureate in Economics, Economics, 7th Edition, 1967.[103]

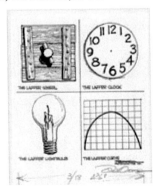

---

[100] http://gregmankiw.blogspot.com/2007/07/on-charlatons-and-cranks.html
[101] http://voices.washingtonpost.com/ezra-klein/2010/08/where_does_the_laffer_curve_be.html
[102] http://voices.washingtonpost.com/ezra-klein/2010/08/where_does_the_laffer_curve_be.html
[103] http://kwasnicki.prawo.uni.wroc.pl/pliki/Perseverance%20of%20Paul%20Samuelson.htm

The upsurge of tax revenues flowing from economic expansion would finance higher levels of local, state, and Federal spending than we would have had without the tax cuts stimulus.
—Walter Heller, Economic Adviser to President Kennedy, on the Kennedy tax cuts, 1970.[104]

Your scheme yields no revenue; it yields nothing but discontent, disorder, disobedience; and such is the state of America, that after wading up to your eyes in blood, you could only end just where you began; that is, to tax where no revenue is found...
—Edmund Burke, Philosopher, arguing against over taxation of the American colonists before Parliament, 1774.[105]

Professor Arthur Laffer, with whose rigidities one can legitimately quarrel, is nonetheless onto something when he says that sluggish performance by workers using creaky industrial equipment and paying high taxes results in low output and, derivatively, smaller returns to the government through the existing tax setup. We have, these days, suffocating tax rates. These give rise to a reduced incentive to work...
—William F. Buckley, founder of the National Review, responding to the Carter Administration's claims that supply economics was "stupid, 1980."[106]

[104] Cited in A. James Meigs' Money Matters: Economics, Markets, Politics, Harper & Row, Publishers, 1972, p. 38)
[105] Alan Blinder, "Thoughts on the Laffer Curve," https://files.stlouisfed.org/files/htdocs/publications/review/81/conf/1981section1-3.pdf
[106] https://home.isi.org/time-action-william-f-buckley-national-review-and-defeat-stagflation

The Laffer Curve:
Voodoo Economics or Lasting Contribution? Part III

Nor should the argument seem strange that taxation may be so high as to defeat its object, and that, given sufficient time to gather the fruits, a reduction of taxation will run a better chance than an increase of balancing the budget. For to take the opposite view today is to resemble a manufacturer who, running at a loss, decides to raise his price, and when his declining sales increase the loss, wrapping himself in the rectitude of plain arithmetic, decides that prudence requires him to raise the price still more—and who, when at last his account is balanced with nought on both sides, is still found righteously declaring that it would have been the act of a gambler to reduce the price when you were already making a loss.
—John Maynard Keynes, The Means to Prosperity, 1933.[107]

High taxes, sometimes by diminishing the consumption of the taxed commodities, and sometimes by encouraging smuggling, frequently afford a smaller revenue to the government than what might be drawn from more moderate taxes.
—Adam Smith, Wealth of Nations, 1776.[108]

Those who argue that government would never operate on the down slope of the Laffer curve [i.e. what we would call the normal range], and who adduce evidence in support, are implicitly adopting a short-run perspective. Those who argue that rate reductions will stimulate supply-side responses sufficient to generate increases in revenues [i.e. in what we would call the prohibitive range], are implicitly adopting a long-run perspective.
—James M. Buchanan, Nobel laureate, and Dwight R. Lee, "Politics, Time, and the Laffer Curve," 1982.[109]

One of "a few of the advances that powered this extraordinary century."
—Time Magazine, "The Century's Greatest Minds," issue on the Laffer curve, 1999.

Supply-side thinking was at the heart of Ronald Reagan's economic policies during his eight-year Administration.
—Wall Street Journal Centennial Edition: People Who Made a Difference, "A Galley of the Greatest: People Who Influenced Our Daily Business," 1989.

One of the most disruptive ideas of the past 85 years.
—Bloomberg Businessweek, "The Dinner Napkin that Changed the U.S. Economy," 2014.[110]

One of "A Dozen Who Shaped the '80s."
—Los Angeles Times, "A Dozen Who Shaped the '80s," 1990.

The creation of the Laffer Curve is a "memorable event."
—Institutional Investor: Silver Anniversary Issue, "The Heroes, Villains, Triumphs, Failures and Other Memorable Events," July 1992.

I know my economic policies are working because they don't call them Reaganomics anymore.[111]
—Ronald Reagan, 1983,

And nearly 200 years ago, one British economist summed up Laffer-Curve effects like this:

Every new tax becomes a new charge on production... A portion of the labour of the country which was before at the disposal of the contributor to the tax, is placed at the disposal of the State, and cannot therefore be employed

[107] John Maynard Keynes, "Keynes and the Laffer Curve," Adam Smith Institute, January 4, 2011.
http://www.adamsmith.org/blog/tax-spending/keynes-and-the-laffer-curve
[108] Smith, Adam, An Inquiry into the Nature and Causes of the Wealth of Nations.
[109] James M. Buchanan and Dwight R. Lee, "Politics, Time, and the Laffer Curve," Journal of Political Economy, Vol. 90, No. 4, Aug. 1982.
[110] https://www.bloomberg.com/news/articles/2014-12-04/laffer-curve-napkin-doodle-launched-supply-side-economics
[111] President Ronald Reagan, "Remarks at the Reagan-Bush Campaign Reunion," November 3, 1983. http://www.presidency.ucsb.edu/ws/?pid=40718

productively. This portion may become so large, that sufficient surplus may not be left to stimulate the exertions of those who usually augment by their savings the capital of the State. Taxation has happily never yet in any free country been carried so far as instantly from year to year to diminish its capital. Such a state of taxation could not be long endured; or if endured, it would be constantly absorbing so much of the annual produce of the country as to occasion the most extensive scene of misery, famine, and depopulation.
—David Ricardo, Economist, 1821.[112]

Whenever politicians come together to cooperate, negotiate, collaborate and compromise, be on your guard, they will most likely find new ways to exploit those whom they govern.

[112] Ricardo, David, On the Principles of Political Economy and Taxation. 1821. Library of Economics and Liberty. 21 June 2017. http://www.econlib.org/library/Ricardo/ricP3a.html

Britain Ruled the Waves by Waiving the Rules / The Thatcher Era Miracle

Don't get wobbly on me now!
— Prime Minister Margaret Thatcher

Lady Thatcher's campaign poster pointing out the tragic consequences of Labour's high taxes, high regulations and excessive spending:

Conservative Party leader Margaret Thatcher became her country's Prime Minister when the Conservatives won the election in May of 1979. She championed lots of clear-eyed policies throughout her 11-plus years in office.

One of her signature accomplishments, under the direct and competent leadership of Secretary of State for Industry Sir Keith Joseph, had to do with the privatization of coal, iron, steel and the railroads from government ownership. Those industries, to this very day, have remained in private hands during both liberal and conservative governments. It only goes to show good policies can be durable.

But Prime Minister Thatcher's crowning achievement, as far as we are concerned, was when she, along with her able Chancellor of the Exchequer Nigel Lawson, cut the highest marginal personal income tax rate from 60% to 40% as of April 6, 1988. The afterburners on the British economy were at full power.

Everyone saw Britain as the ideal place for capital investments. Thatcher's tax rate cut in the UK increased the after-tax rate of return on UK located assets enormously. Capital was lined up on the UK border trying to get into the UK, as opposed to leaving the UK.

Capital flows into the UK are measured as capital inflows as well as trade deficits. From early 1987, the UK's trade balance went from a rough balance to a deficit (i.e. capital surplus) of almost 4% of GDP in late 1988/early 1989. This is exactly the Sidney Alexander or absorption approach to the trade balance. The flood of capital seeking to profit from good tax policy poured into the UK, creating a huge capital surplus and trade deficit.

Let me tell you how it will be
There's one for you, nineteen for me
Cos I'm the taxman, yeah, I'm the tax man
— First verse of Taxman, The Beatles

Economic Ignorance Leads to Political Rejection—The UK Example

UK Inflation, Mark per Pound Exchange Rate and UK Top Marginal Personal Income Tax Rate
(inflation is year-over-year % change in monthly RPI, exchange rate is end of month, Jan-83 to Jan-93)

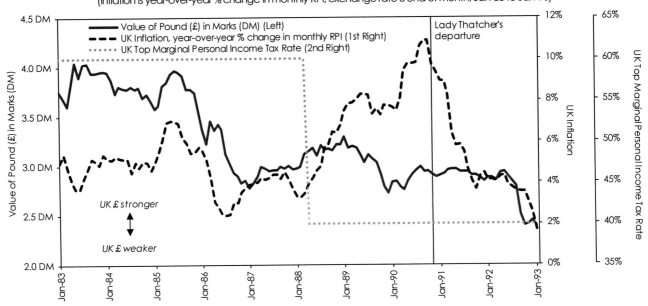

Source: UK Office of National Statistics, Bloomberg

But instead of allowing the British pound to revalue as it should have done, the UK government took it upon itself to approximately fix the British pound to the German mark. The logic was as simple as it was wrong. The UK government thought that fixing the pound to the German mark would maintain British goods' competitiveness, which is an attempt to effectively devalue the pound. Unfortunately, nothing could have been further from the truth. British goods were going to become non-competitive by hook or by crook to allow capital to enter the country.

As shown in the above chart, from early 1988, British inflation rose from a little below 4% per annum to well over 10% in late 1990, destroying along with it one of the best governments the UK has ever seen. Prime Minister Thatcher was forced to resign her post as Prime Minister in November of 1990 as a result of the huge political backlash to domestic inflation. The high inflation never would have happened if the pound had been allowed to appreciate. International economics does matter.

> *Should five per cent appear too small*
> *Be thankful I don't take it all*
> *Cos I'm the taxman, yeah, I'm the tax man*
> *— Second verse of Taxman, The Beatles*

Complex Error Replaces Simple Truth: More Recent Comings and Goings of UK Taxes

In April 2010, UK Labour Prime Minister Gordon Brown increased the highest tax rate on income from 40% to 50%, the first increase in 30 years. The Exchequer under Labour, led by Prime Minister Brown claimed that the new tax would yield £2.5 billion additional tax revenue. In 2012, HM Revenue and Customs published *"The Exchequer effect of the 50 per cent additional rate of income tax"* to wit.[113] What follows printed in red are direct quotes from the Exchequer Report.

Trends in top rates of (central government) income tax in the UK

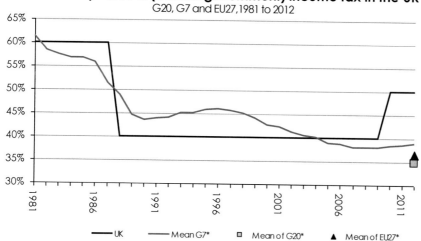

If you drive a car, I'll tax the street
If you try to sit, I'll tax your seat
If you get too cold, I'll tax the heat
If you take a walk, I'll tax your feet
— Third verse of Taxman, The Beatles

Sources: OECD, Eurostat, HM Treasury

• The modelling (Mirrlees Review) suggests the underlying behavioural response was greater than estimated previously in Budget 2009 and in March Budget 2010, decreasing the pre-behavioural yield by at least 83 per cent. This result…suggests the additional rate is a highly distortionary form of taxation.

• The conclusion that can be drawn from the Self Assessment data is…that the underlying yield from the additional rate is much lower than originally forecast (yielding around £1 billion or less), and that it is quite possible that it could be negative.

• Evidence from the U.S. suggests that the behavioural responses could be even higher, with an even lower yield.

• International labour mobility has increased in the last 15 to 20 years as both legal impediments and general migration costs have been reduced, which means the adverse effect of high rates

---

[113] HM Revenue & Customs, "The Exchequer effect of the 50 per cent additional rate of income tax," p.2, March 2012.

on personal taxation on both inward and outward migration to the UK and tax revenues can be significant.

• The Exchequer impacts of changes in migration can be considerable as the Exchequer loses the tax on the individuals' entire income rather than just the income subject to the additional rate.

• They (the tax increases) still result in a significant direct Exchequer impact, and are still wasteful from an economic point of view as they require individuals to spend more time and resources tax planning, resulting in other economic distortions.

• Total income of the affected group in 2009-10 and 2010-11 combined was £203 billion. This was 5 percent below the combined total of £212 billion for the preceding two years, even though:

    o Based on the historical average, this group's incomes would have grown by 26 percent over a two year period; and

    o Incomes in 2009-10 included incomes brought forward from 2011-12 and beyond.

• The extent of the shortfall in tax liabilities in 2010-11 is such that it is relatively difficult to construct a plausible scenario in which there was not a substantial underlying behavioural loss in that year.

• Any behavioural responses that reduce disposable incomes could result in a reduction in expenditure and corresponding indirect tax revenues. Estimating the proportion of any overall response that relates to real changes that affect incomes (rather than responses such as increased tax planning and avoidance which do not) is difficult as most academic studies only estimate the overall behavioural response. However, considering studies which do attempt to breakdown the behavioural response suggest that between one-third and one-half of the response comes from genuine reductions in disposable income.

• The results can only be considered an estimate of the yield in a very short term and as such may be higher than the long term yield, particularly as some behavioural responses such as the possibility that those affected might leave the UK may take place over a number of years.

• High tax rates in the UK make its tax system less competitive and make it a less attractive place to start, finance and grow a business. The longer the additional rate remains in place the more people are likely to consider it a permanent feature of the UK tax system and the more damaging it would be for competitiveness.

What is definitely flattering is that in this March 2012 report, there is a whole section on Laffer Curves (pg. 51, Sections A22 and A23). They should have asked Arthur Laffer ahead of time what the affects would be. We guess Prime Minister Gordon Brown misplaced Arthur's phone number.

Why is Everyone Investing in Ireland—The Capital is Always Dublin

Irish Corporate and Personal Income Tax Rates and Inflation Differential: Ireland vs. Eurozone
(monthly, Jan-96 to Jan-08, inflation is differential of indexed monthly CPI Jan-96=100)

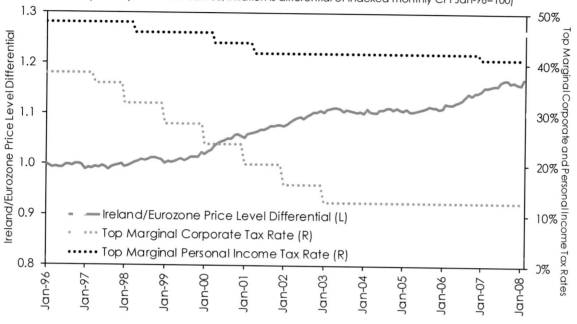

Source: OECD, Eurostat, Irish Taxation Institute

Ireland experienced firsthand the perils of fixed exchange rates when pro-growth economic policies were put into place during the late 1990s and early 2000s. Arthur Laffer wrote at the time:

> *The Irish pound is not free to appreciate, and therefore Irish prices have to rise to bring balance between Ireland and the rest of Europe… the inflation in Ireland results from the Irish pound's linkage to the euro and from a change in the relative prices of Irish located goods versus foreign goods. This change in Ireland's "terms-of-trade" is a direct consequence of Ireland's fantastic tax cuts and pro-growth economic policies. Foreigners want to invest in Ireland. Ireland's capital surplus is her trade deficit and to induce a trade deficit Irish goods had to become non-competitive in the global marketplace. Because the exchange rate has not been free to move all of the adjustment has taken place in the increase in the prices of Irish goods. This is Ireland's problem.[114]*

Instead of allowing the Irish pound to float freely, Ireland decided to keep the fixed euro-Irish pound (also called the punt) exchange rate and eventually adopt the euro currency fully. As a result, Ireland experienced significantly higher inflation than the rest of Europe all the way through the mid-2000s. And of course, true to form, Ireland's government collapsed and their pro-growth agenda came to an abrupt halt. *Erin Go Bragh.*

[114] Arthur B. Laffer, "The Luck of the Irish: Why Ireland Should Punt the Euro," Laffer Associates, August 1, 2000.

Cumulative Real GDP: Ireland vs. Eurozone
(annual, 1997-2015, indexed 100=1997)

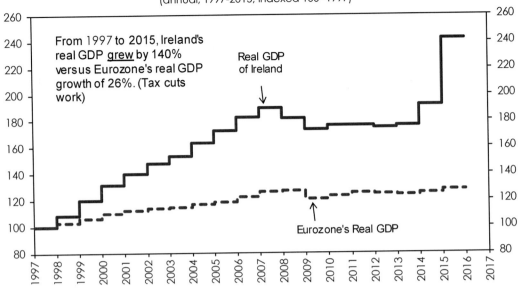

From 1997 to 2015, Ireland's real GDP grew by 140% versus Eurozone's real GDP growth of 26%. (Tax cuts work)

Real GDP of Ireland

Eurozone's Real GDP

Source: Eurostat

The Dragon Returns: The Story of China

It takes a Ph.D. in economics not to be able to understand the obvious.
— *Irving Kristol*

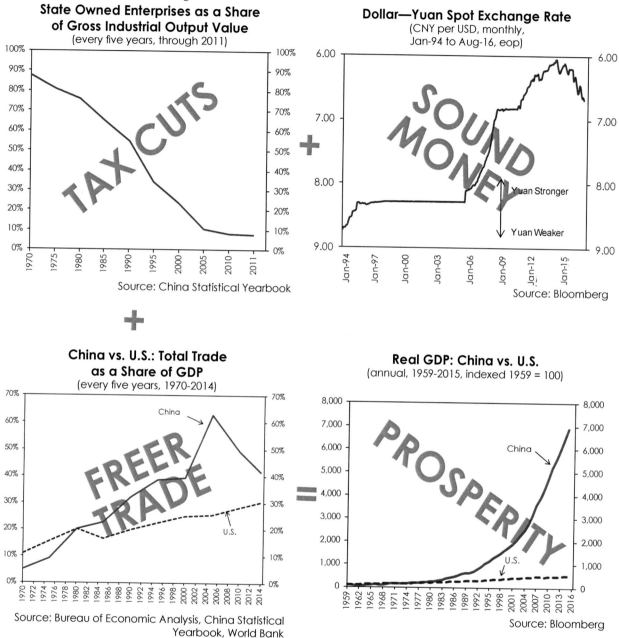

State Owned Enterprises as a Share of Gross Industrial Output Value (every five years, through 2011)

Source: China Statistical Yearbook

Dollar—Yuan Spot Exchange Rate (CNY per USD, monthly, Jan-94 to Aug-16, eop)

Yuan Stronger / Yuan Weaker

Source: Bloomberg

China vs. U.S.: Total Trade as a Share of GDP (every five years, 1970-2014)

China / U.S.

Source: Bureau of Economic Analysis, China Statistical Yearbook, World Bank

Real GDP: China vs. U.S. (annual, 1959-2015, indexed 1959 = 100)

China / U.S.

Source: Bloomberg

From 1959 through 2016, China's real GDP grew 69 fold (6900%) versus U.S. real GDP growth of 540%, or 5.4 fold.

Since the late 1970s, China has seized upon three major pillars of supply-side economics: tax cuts, sound money and free trade. By importing supply-side economics to the world's largest population, to quote *our* good friend Bill Shiebler, *"China has presided over the biggest anti-poverty program in the history of the world, bringing tens of millions of people out of poverty on an annual basis for decades."*

113

The Khaldun-Laffer Curve for Turkey

Figure 1: Turkey vs. European Union: Excess Real GDP Growth

(annual, Real GDP: 2005-2014, Emp: 2005-2015, indexed 2005=100)

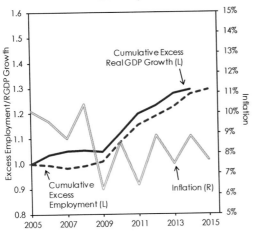

Source: Eurostat, OECD, Turkish Ministry of Finance

Figure 2: Turkey: Corporate Tax Rate and Corporate Tax Revenues as a Share of GDP

(annual, 1998-2014)

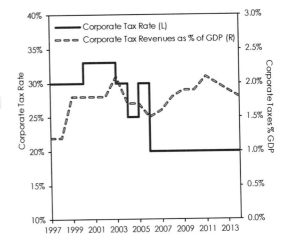

Source: OECD, Trading Economics

Figure 3: A Real Miracle Turkey Government Debt-to-GDP Ratio Down, EU Up

(annual, 2002-2015)

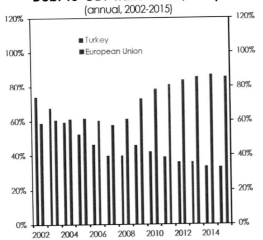

Source: Eurostat, Trading Economics

Figure 4: Turkey Privatization Revenues

(annual, 2004-2015, $ billions)

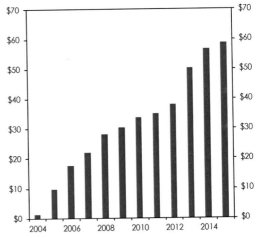

Source: Turkish Privatization Administration, World Bank

Turkey has had explosive growth in its economy and employment over the past 15 years, and for good reasons: supply-side economics. In Figure 1, we show Turkey's employment and real GDP relative to the European Union, with the 2005 values indexed to 100 in order to easily demonstrate the growth of these metrics. In Figures 2 and 3, we show Turkey's corporate tax rate and tax revenues vis-à-vis Turkey's GDP, as well as Turkey's and the EU's debt-to-GDP ratios. And lastly, in Figure 4, we have Turkey's annual privatization revenues. Is it any wonder Turkey owns its growth? Tax cuts are an equal opportunity employer.

…the Khaldun-Laffer curve, on the basis of personal income tax by making use annual time-series data for Turkey for the period 1970-2015. The findings of the paper confirm the validity of the Khaldun-Laffer curve hypothesis. In addition, we infer that the optimal tax rate that maximizes the tax revenue generated from personal income taxation in Turkey is 15.03 percent.[115]

---

[115] Huseyin Sen, Ayse Kaya, and Zeynep Burcu Bulut-Cevik, "The Khaldun-Laffer Curve Revisited: A Personal Income Tax-Based Analysis for Turkey," Munich Personal RePEc Archive, April 10, 2017. https://mpra. ub.uni-muenchen.de/78850/1/MPRA_paper_78850.pdf

But What About Sweden?—Joel Citron

The Swedish honesty has been a matter of pride for me and my generation. I now believe that through a system of bad laws we are becoming hucksters. Of all the inadequacies of our income tax laws, the most serious aspect is that it directly invites us to commit tax evasion and tax fraud.[116]
— *Gunnar Myrdal, Economics Nobel Laureate, 1978*

In the early 1990s, the Swedish banking system and economy all but collapsed. Starting with the great tax reform of 1991, Sweden has spent the past 25 years dismantling its once socialist system, a process that continues to this day.[117]

The process lowered marginal tax rates from 80% to 50% in the early 1990s and simplified the tax code—capital gains taxes were lowered and dividend and interest income became taxable as capital. In 2015, the highest marginal tax rate (local and central) was 60%, and capital gains, interest income and dividends were all taxed at 30%.

Labor Force Participation Rate (15-64 year olds)
(annual, U.S.: 1960-2015, Sweden: 1963-2015)

Source: OECD

The 1.5% annual wealth tax, the inheritance tax (estate tax) and the gift tax were eliminated. Today, you can pass assets to your family without paying any taxes. What you earned is yours. As a result, people with wealth have come back to Sweden.

Real estate taxes are virtually nonexistent with a ceiling of several hundred dollars per year. Value-added-taxes (VAT) remain high, and the effective corporate tax rate is somewhere between 22-25%.

Unions have gone from adversarial with management to collaborative. Swedish business formation has sky-rocketed over the last 25 years compared to the prior 25 year period, making Sweden/Stockholm one of the top high tech countries in the world. Sweden has also been able to move from a pension system (social security) of defined benefits to defined contributions. That is a huge deal.

---

[116] Gunnar Myrdal, "Dags for ett bättre skattesystem (Time for a better tax system)," Taxes, p. 500, 1982
[117] Thanks to Joel Citron, our ever-faithful source on the truth about Sweden.

Deregulatory reforms have unleashed creativity and competition. There is now universal school choice, as well as a growing number of private medical practices and hospitals.

Finally, there is a debate to undo the minimum wage and move to a system where either the employer is relieved of payroll taxes or the individual is exempt from paying taxes.

Sweden has kept its own currency, the krona, and has a separate immigration system from the EU. As a result, the krona has performed very well and, because Sweden did not join with the EU in the stimulus spending program in 2009, the Great Recession was virtually non-existent in Sweden.

> *When I think about capitalism I think about all the businesses that were started because we have the opportunity and the freedom to do that and to make a good living for themselves and their families... We are not Denmark...I love Denmark. We are the United States of America.*
> *— Hillary Clinton, 2016 Presidential Democratic Primary Debate, October 13, 2015*

Sayonara Japan

**Japan: 5 Year Real GDP Growth Annualized vs.
General Government Expenditures as a Share of GDP**
(RGDP: 5-year Q4 to Q4 rolling growth rates, 4Q55-4Q60 to 4Q10-4Q15;
Expenditures: annual, historical 1970-2014, 2015 estimate)

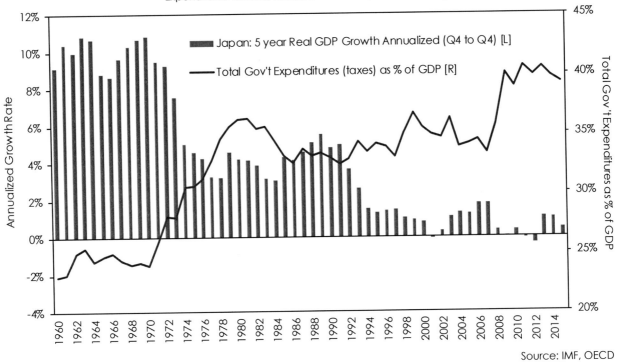

Source: IMF, OECD

In his book *The Way the World Works*, our dear late friend Jude Wanniski wrote this about Japan circa 1980:

> "*The most remarkable facet of Japanese tax policies since 1950 is the consistency of the reductions. In every year since 1950, the government has cut marginal tax rates on personal and/or business income, either directly through rates or indirectly through tax preferences ("loop-holes"). Budget surpluses, real or anticipated, are thus given back to the private sector to spend. Economic growth has been spectacular, with GNP rising from $16 billion in 1952 to $300 billion in 1972.*"

> "*…[from 1950 to 1974] Japan cut rates by roughly 11 percent annually, and at the end of the process revenues were $63 billion, or four times the nations GNP at the start of the process.*" [118]

What a difference now. The chart above shows the substantial increase in Japan's government spending moving in lockstep with the outsized decline in Japan's real GDP growth. Even the variations in the growth in government spending correspond uncannily closely to movements in real GDP growth, only in the opposite direction.

---

[118] Jude Wanniski, The Way the World Works, 4th Edition, pp. 207, 2001.

No matter how many times we invoke Milton Friedman's name, it still brings back warm memories of a good friend and a great economist. Here again we are reminded of Milton Friedman's view that government spending is taxation, only now in the context of Japan's economy during the 46 years from 1970 through 2016. Follow Japanese government spending as a share of GDP and Japanese economic growth and the negative relationship is crystal clear. And then realize that in August 2016, the recently reelected Abe government in Japan announced a government spending stimulus package with a total value of ¥28 trillion ($274 billion) over several years that includes: ¥7.5 trillion ($73 billion) in direct spending, cash handouts of ¥15,000 ($147) each to 22 million low-income people, increased spending on infrastructure projects and, in an effort to address the nation's labor shortage, funding for the creation of more child-care facilities for working parents and to help employers provide longer maternity leave.[119] SAYONARA JAPAN.

---

[119] Mitsuru Obe, "Japan's Shinzo Abe Fires Stimulus Gun, Again," The Wall Street Journal, August 2, 2016. http://on.wsj.com/2aRIVW0

Was ist Den Los?

In Jude Wanniski's book *The Way the World Works*, he had this to say about Germany's economic miracle of the 1950s and 1960s:

> *It was this systematic lowering of unnecessarily high tax rates that produced the German economic miracle, just as the Mellon tax cuts boomed the U.S. economy in the 1920s. As national income rose in Germany throughout the 1950s, so did revenues, providing the government the wherewithal to construct a social support system as well as a powerful national defense system.[120]*

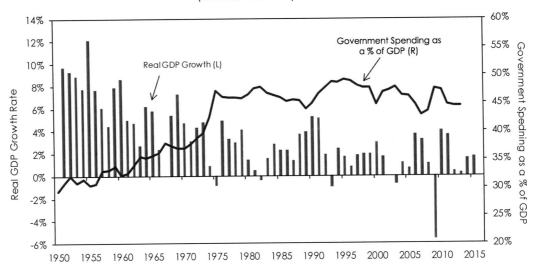

Real GDP Growth Rate vs. Government Spending as a Share of GDP
(annual, 1950-2015)

Source: FRED, Berlin Social Science Center, OECD

The two major economic miracles (in German it's called "Das Wirtschaftswunder") of the post-World War II era are Germany and Japan. In both cases, taxes, as shown by government spending as a share of GDP, started off very low with rapid economic growth and, as the years passed, government spending/taxes increased and growth tapered off. Just look at the chart above, which shows a striking relationship between government spending/taxation and the retardation of growth.

And then, as Germany entered the modern era, Jude Wanniski saw clearly the dangers confronting the country:

> *To the Keynesian, who sees no difference between tax rates and tax revenues, nothing has changed in Germany. The government was getting 35 percent of national income sixty years ago and is still getting 35 percent of national income. The difference, of course, is that with correct rates, Germany's national income has risen tenfold.[121]*

---

[120] Jude Wanniski, The Way the World Works, 4th Edition, pp. 205, 2001.
[121] Ibid.

Here's What a Tax System Should Be

KISS, according to James Carville, President Clinton's key advisor and muse, is: *Keep it simple, stupid!*

Isle of Man: Tax Guide[122]

Income Tax Rates

Resident Individuals	2015/2016
Single Person	
£1-£10,500	10%
Over £10,500	20%
Married Couples (Joint)	
£1-£21,000	10%
Over £21,000	20%
Tax Cap (max. tax liability)	£125,000
(if jointly assessed)	£250,000
Companies	**2015/2016**
Banking businesses	10%
Manx land & property	20%
All other income	0%

* There is no Capital Gains Tax or Inheritance Tax

Capital Allowances

	2015/2016
Plant & Machinery:	
First year allowance	100%
Writing-down allowance	25%
Industrial buildings:	
Initial allowance	100%
Writing-down allowance	4%
Tourist premises:	
Initial allowance	100%
Writing-down allowance	10%
Agricultural buildings:	
Initial allowance	100%
Writing-down allowance	10%

National Insurance Contributions

Class 1 Employed—not contracted out—on all earnings per week:		
2015/2016	**Employees**	**Employers**
£0-£120	NIL / 0%	NIL / 0% / 12.8%
£120-£784	11%	12.8%
Over £784	1%	12.8%
Class 4 earnings related on taxable profits		
£6,136-£40,768 p.a.	8%	8%
Over £40,768 p.a.	1%	1%

Hong Kong Tax Rates[123]

Tax Bracket (HKD)	Total tax on income below bracket	Tax rate on income in bracket
0-40,000	800	2%
40,001-80,000	2,800	7%
80,001-120,000	4,800	12%
Over 120,001	0	17%
Other Taxes		
VAT	None	None
Capital Gains / Investment Income	None	None
Social Security	None	None
Estate / Gift	None	None

[122] "Isle of Man Tax Guide 2015/2016," Grant Thornton. http://www.grantthornton.co.im/Docs/Isle-of-Man-Tax-Guide-2015-2016.aspx
[123] "Hong Kong SAR Tax Profile," KPMG, July 2016. https://home.kpmg.com/content/dam/kpmg/xx/pdf/2016/10/country-tax-profile-hong-kong.pdf

Section IX –
Government Policy Actions: Energy

In the 1970s logical thinking in politics went off the tracks to say the least. In August of 1971 President Nixon devalued the U.S. dollar, put on a 10% import surcharge and initiated the Job Development Credit, which was a 7% investment tax credit for new investments excluding foreign made investment. But most of all he imposed wage and price controls for all products and prices save raw materials and interest rates. These controls were reversed in 1973 save for oil and gasoline products.

Falling CO2 Emissions Doesn't Mean Lower GDP

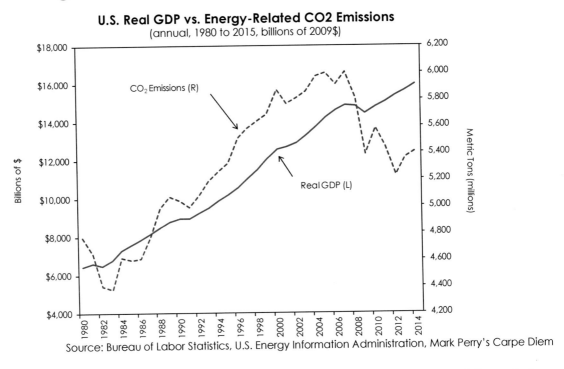

U.S. Real GDP vs. Energy-Related CO2 Emissions
(annual, 1980 to 2015, billions of 2009$)

Source: Bureau of Labor Statistics, U.S. Energy Information Administration, Mark Perry's Carpe Diem

With all the brouhaha surrounding global warming and the lack of effort to restrain CO2 emissions in the United States, the above graph contains one measure of the detrimental environmental consequences of using carbon products. Pretty amazing.

Despite not signing the Kyoto Protocol, in 2015, U.S. energy-related carbon dioxide emissions have tumbled and were 12% below the 2005 levels and real GDP was 15% larger than it was in 2005. On a per-dollar of gross domestic product (GDP) basis in 2015, compared to 2005, the United States used 15% less energy per unit of real GDP and produced 23% fewer energy-related CO2 emissions per unit of real GDP.[124]

There have been huge environmental/economic changes that have occurred in our lifetimes—for example, pollution is way down. One of us (Arthur Laffer) as a boy was raised in the 1940s and 1950s on the shores of Lake Erie. Today, it is truly a miracle that Lake Erie is clean. The Cuyahoga River no longer catches on fire; even the Hudson River in New York is back to its pristine state. A running joke used to be a charcoal grey postcard entitled, "L.A. on a Clear Day." Over the 30 year period ending in 2006, the percentage of days per year in the Los Angeles area that violated federal air quality standards had fallen from over 50% to less than 10%. In addition, the number of federal "health advisory" days per year in California had fallen from 166 to 11 over the same period.[125]

[124] "U.S. energy-related carbon dioxide emissions in 2015 are 12% below their 2005 levels," U.S. Energy Information Agency, May 9, 2015. http://www.eia.gov/todayinenergy/detail.cfm?id=26152
[125] Arthur B. Laffer, "The Condition of Our Nation," Laffer Associates, May 8, 2006.

The Truth About Air Quality

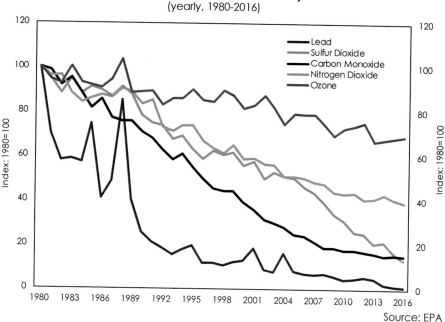

National Ambient Air Quality
(yearly, 1980-2016)

Legend: Lead, Sulfur Dioxide, Carbon Monoxide, Nitrogen Dioxide, Ozone

Source: EPA

The U.S. withdraw from the Paris Agreement has been used to label the U.S. as anti-environment. The chart above gives us a fresh perspective.

Air pollutants have been on a steady downward trend since 1980. These five pollutants represented in the graph have decreased in concentration by approximately 73% as a whole over the span of 36 years, in spite of increases in population, energy use, and vehicle miles traveled.[126] Carbon monoxide is down 85%, lead is down 99%, nitrogen dioxide 62%, ozone 31%, and sulfur dioxide 87%. Also across this time period, total emissions of the six[127] principle air pollutants dropped by 67%. Positive progress is being made in all directions.

The EPA credits these air improvements to the Clean Air Act of 1963, which was the first federal legislation addressing air pollution. The act has been frequently amended since and is evidently very effective in fulfilling its purposes for the U.S.

[Withdraw from the Paris Agreement] is an unprecedented forfeiture of American leadership which will cost us influence, cost us jobs, and invite other countries to walk away from solving humanity's most existential crisis.[128]
—John Kerry, Secretary of State when Paris Agreement was negotiated.

We're getting out. And we will start to renegotiate and we'll see if there's a better deal. If we can, great. If we can't, that's fine.....As someone who cares deeply about our environment, I cannot in good conscience support a deal which punishes the United States. The Paris accord is very unfair at the highest level to the United States.[129]
— President Donald Trump, on the Paris Agreement.

I've come here personally, as the leader of the world's largest economy and the second-largest emitter, to say that the United States of America not only recognizes our role in creating this problem, we embrace our responsibility to do something about it.[130]
—Barack Obama, first session on the Paris Agreement

[126] "Our Nation's Air," U.S. Environmental Protection Agency, 2017. https://gispub.epa.gov/air/trendsreport/2017/#effects
[127] Includes particulate matter, which is not represented in above graph on air quality based on air concentrations.
[128] Madeline Conway, "Obama slams Trump for leaving Paris climate agreement," POLITICO, June 1 2017. https://www.politico.com/story/2017/06/01/barack-obama-slams-donald-trump-paris-climate-239032
[129] Kevin Liptak and Jim Acosta, "Trump on Paris accord: 'We're getting out'," CNN, June 2 2017. http://www.cnn.com/2017/06/01/politics/trump-paris-climate-decision/index.html
[130] Barack Obama, "Remarks by President Obama at the First Session of COP21," November 20 2015. https://obamawhitehouse.archives.gov/the-press-office/2015/11/30/remarks-president-obama-first-session-cop21

President Jimmy Carter's Oil Fiasco

Spot Price of Oil vs Quality of Operational Rigs
(1973-1986)

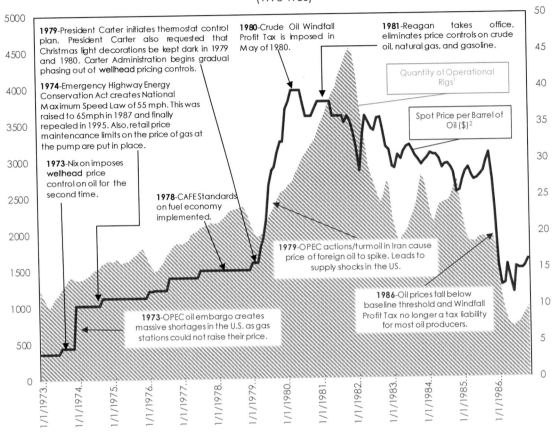

Source: EIA, St. Louis Federal Reserve

Throughout the 1970s, the Organization of Petroleum Exporting Countries (OPEC) limited oil production including a U.S. oil embargo in 1973, which when combined with the U.S. dollar depreciation caused the price of a barrel to rise ten-fold.

Government rationing of gas and oil started under Nixon's price controls with a ban on gas price increases. Rationing for the right to purchase gasoline included an odd-even license plate system. Wellhead price controls were capped at $5.25/barrel for oil, and natural gas was, also, subjected to wellhead price controls.

A "gas guzzler tax" was placed on cars (1980), a reduction in the national speed limit to 55 miles per hour (1974-1987)), a ban on outdoor Christmas lights (1979-1980), a requirement for airlines to recirculate air in planes (1980), the implementation of year-round daylight savings time (1974-1975), and a voluntary policy urging stores and public buildings to turn the thermostat to a chilly 65 degrees in winter and no lower than a sweaty 78 in summer (1979-1981).

126

A windfall profits tax to prevent oil companies from profiting from the OPEC price spikes was legislated (1980). The Corporate Average Fuel Economy (CAFE) standards penalizing car manufacturers were introduced (1978). The Carter Administration also made a $2 billion "investment' in something called the Synthetic Fuels Corporation. It was closed down in 1982.

From 1971 to 1980, U.S. oil production fell from 11 to 9 million barrels a day. Oil price controls brought new drilling in the U.S. to a standstill. Price controls also increased U.S. oil consumption from 15 to 19 million barrels a day from 1970 through 1978 causing the wrenching 1978 to 1981 energy shortage. Imports of foreign oil rose from 1.3 to 6.6 million barrels a day from 1970 to 1977.

In late January 1981, as one of the first official acts of his presidency, President Reagan issued an executive order removing all natural gas, crude oil, and gasoline price controls. The number of rigs operating in the U.S. immediately jumped 30 percent to record highs while oil production in the "Lower 48" increased for the first time since 1970.

By the end of 1981, oil consumption in the U.S. dropped by 20 percent. The American car industry shifted from large, long wheelbase rear-wheel drive vehicles to much smaller, lighter front-wheel drive vehicles. After the lifting of price controls, the imported share of oil was down to 45 percent. By January 1982 U.S. oil production rose by 50 percent above 1980 levels and by 100 percent above 1979 levels. Economics works.

Oil

Today, hundreds of years after the Industrial Revolution began, most of the human population is dependent on fossil fuels for 80 to 90 percent of its energy supply. That will surely be the case at least for many decades.[131]
— Stephen Moore, *Fueling Freedom*, 2016

U.S. Oil Production and Consumption vs. Real Price of Oil
(annual, 1950-2015; Production & Consumption: BTUs per dollar of Real GDP (2009$); Price: average, 2015$)

Source: EIA, U.S. Bureau of Economic Analysis, Laffer Associates

From 1950 through 2015, petroleum consumption in the U.S., as measured in the British Thermal Units (BTUs) per dollar of real GDP, has fallen by 65% and follows the inverse pattern of oil prices as predicted by price theory—i.e. higher prices mean less consumption and lower prices mean higher consumption. Over this same period, U.S. production of crude oil, again measured in BTUs per dollar of real GDP, has fallen by 77%.

Actor James Dean striking oil in the movie *Giant*

The reasons why decontrol would leave wholesale prices unchanged have nothing to do with the effectiveness of the Government's attempts to control crude oil prices. The United States market quite simply is integrated with the world petroleum market. United States distributors of gasoline, heating oil and diesel fuel compete directly on a global basis for supplies. This competition assures that United States wholesale prices before taxes are equilibrated with world prices. Petroleum derivative product prices are no different. If price controls held United States wholesale prices below world prices, American buyers would be shut out of the world market place. Domestic "shortages," which have invariably followed effective price controls, would be unavoidable.

United States refined-product markets are integrated with world markets. Domestic wholesalers are forced by the discipline of competition to bring their prices into line with world prices. This in turn renders ineffective attempts to reduce domestic refined-product prices by controlling domestic crude-oil prices.[132]
— Charles W. Kadlec and Arthur B. Laffer, 1979

---

[131] Stephen Moore and Kathleen Hartnett White, Fueling Freedom, "Introduction," pg. xiv, 2016.
[132] Charles W. Kadlec and Arthur B. Laffer, "Does Oil Decontrol Mean Lower Prices?" The New York Times, September 2, 1979.

What Happened to Peak Oil?

At least fifty trillion dollars' worth of recoverable energy—the greatest storehouse of treasure in history—lies beneath federal lands and federal water. Drilling for these resources will create millions of new American jobs and could increase the growth rate of GDP from 2 percent to 4 percent or more.[133]
— Stephen Moore, Fueling Freedom, 2016

We could use up all of the proven reserves of oil in the entire world by the end of the next decade...The energy crisis...will be the 'moral equivalent of war'.
—Jimmy Carter, 1977

World Oil Reserves in Years of Usage
(annual, 1980-2014)

Source: BP

Throughout our lifetimes (which we both expect will last quite a while longer) Chicken Little has been screaming that "the sky is falling." And, Chicken Little's next of kin, oil experts, have ominously warned that the world is running out of oil and Armageddon is nigh.

Judging from the above chart of the number of years' worth of oil in known reserves, these purveyors of doom need to go home and be quiet.

Everyone relies on oil. In 1980, for example, consumption expenditures on oil—both imported and domestically produced—comprised a full 5.3% of U.S. GDP. While expenditures have come down from those heights, the U.S. nonetheless is still a huge net importer of oil. In 2015, the U.S. imported 2.52 billion barrels of oil net and spent 0.7% of its GDP doing so.

[133] Stephen Moore and Kathleen Hartnett White, Fueling Freedom, "Introduction," pg. xiv, 2016.

Government Can and Has Gotten It Right Many Times—Part III

The rust brown runoff from the Cuyahoga River flows into the blue waters of Lake Erie.

Example #5 Cuyahoga River and Lake Erie

Anyone who falls in the Cuyahoga does not drown. He decays.
—Cleveland citizen quoted in Time Magazine, August 1, 1969

Cuyahoga on Fire: A fire on June 22, 1969 caught the attention of Time Magazine, and in turn, the entire nation.

• The Problem: The growth of the 19th and 20th centuries was borne by the waterways which transported goods, people, and unfortunately, waste. The Cuyahoga River became so polluted with industrial waste that it caught fire 13 times![134]

• The Solution: Due in part to the 1969 Cuyahoga fire, Congress passed the National Environment Protection Act (NEPA) in 1970, which led to the creation of the Environmental Protection Agency (EPA) and the Clean Water Act, the last of which mandated that water be clean enough for humans and fish to safely swim in, and devoted funds to cleanup efforts. By the 2000s, the Cuyahoga River and Lake Erie met or exceeded most EPA benchmarks.

Example #6: Acid Rain

• The Problem: Acid rain is a broad term that includes any form of precipitation with acidic components, such as sulfuric or nitric acid that fall to the ground from the atmosphere in wet or dry forms. This can include rain, snow, fog, hail or even dust that is acidic.[135]

This statute of George Washington was erected in New York City in 1944 (left). 50 years later, erosion from acid rain left the Sage of Mount Vernon unrecognizable (right).

• The Solution: Enable economic principles, property rights, to work their magic. The Acid Rain Program (ARP) of the 1990 Clean Air Act used a market-based system to achieve emission reductions, meet environmental goals, and improve human health. The improvement has been so great that acid rain is no longer a topic of conversation.

---

[134] Source: Adler, Jonathan H., "Fables of the Cuyahoga: Reconstructing a History of Environmental Protection" (2002). Faculty Publications. 191.
[135] Source: United states Environmental Protection Agency

Advertisement touting the health benefits of cigarette smoking, 1881.

Example #7: Reduced Prevalence of Smoking

• The Problem: The dramatic increase in deaths due to cancer among adults in the 1940s and beyond.

• The Solution: In 1964, the U.S. Surgeon General released a landmark first-of-its kind report on the harmful health effects associated with tobacco smoking. Drawing upon over 7,000 scientific studies, the report tied smoking to lung and laryngeal cancer.[136]

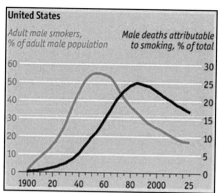

Data from the Centers for Disease Control illustrating the prevalence of smoking and smoking related deaths among the adult male population in the U.S. from 1900-2012, and forecasts into 2025. Reprinted in The Economist.

The Surgeon General's report dominated the headlines and at the time was one of the biggest stories of 1964. The Federal Cigarette Labeling and Advertising Act of 1965 and the Public Health Cigarette Smoking Act of 1969 limited how cigarette companies could promote tobacco products. Since then smoking rates among adults and teens have been reduced by half (see chart to above).

---

[136] Source: "History of the Surgeon General's Reports on Smoking and Health," Centers for Disease Control. https://www.cdc.gov/tobacco/data_statistics/sgr/history/index.htm

Section X – Government Policy Actions: State and Local

Individual U.S. states exercise considerable autonomy in implementing economic policies. As a consequence, measures of relative success and failure also vary considerably. In the field of International Economics, labor is assumed to be immobile and thus arbitrage across national boundaries occurs through trade in goods and services (quantities) and through changes in the terms of trade (inflation-adjusted exchange rates). Measures of success or failure in international economics include income per capita, the unemployment rate, and other measures of the standard of living. When labor is freely and, relatively speaking, costlessly mobile across state boundaries, however, as is the case in the United States, measures such as income per capita or unemployment rates no longer make sense. Any measure of prosperity where the number of people is in the denominator, such as income per capita or the unemployment rate, makes little or no sense when people can move to where income or jobs are located, or the jobs and income can move to where people are located.

In the case of the 50 U.S. states, increases in income per capita, for example, can occur when a state attracts income faster than it attracts people or when that state repels people faster than it repels income. While income per capita may increase in both cases, the welfare implications are diametrically opposed. Measures of movement of the factors of production, income, goods, and people are the appropriate metrics of measuring welfare when it comes to each of the 50 states of the United States, not income per capita or unemployment rates.

State and local governments have a great deal of leeway to tax, spend, regulate, and oversee economic activities as long as their voters choose to permit them to do so and as long as the Commerce Clause of the Constitution and the Privileges and Immunities Clause of the Constitution are not violated. And, with the powerful presence of those clauses, people, goods, and services also have their constitutionally given rights to locate when and where they wish.

Given the trivial differences in language as spoken in the various states, the existence of a common currency, and the fairly similar social customs of the various state populations, as well as the contiguous nature of all save two of our states, in-migration and out-migration are as painless and costless as possible. The economic integration of the 50 states truly is as close to a perfect economic union as can be conceived. As such, the central theme of this section of the Template is simply to answer the following questions: Do state and local government economic policies redistribute income, or do they redistribute people?

The differences among the states with respect to taxes, school choice, right-to-work laws, minimum wage, and cultural factors as well, indicate that blue states are getting bluer and red states are getting redder. There is also a huge drift in the overall economic performance toward red states.

Politics have consequences. To overuse a cliché, America is at a crossroads, and nowhere is the battleground raging more than it is in almost every state capital in this nation. Here is the story told by states.

There is a general rule that if you see an expert on television a lot, he or she probably isn't much of an expert—if nothing else, real experts are too busy doing research to be on that many shows. And the qualities that make for good TV are not closely related to those that make for good research. This observation is not unique to economics; for example, Stephen Hawking, whose "A Brief History of Time" was a best seller and who has been the subject of a number of adoring documentaries, is not the world's leading physicist.
— Paul Krugman, Peddling Prosperity, 1995.

Stephen Hawking is the Lucasian Professor of Physics at Oxford University and recipient of the prestigious Wolf Prize in Mathematics.

PAUL KRUGMAN ON POTENTIAL TRUMP MEDIA VENTURE

What If? States and Cities in 2015 Would Have Had $581 Billion More in Their Coffers

Thus, the taxpayer is abridged of his enjoyments, the producer of his profits, and the public exchequer of its receipts. This is the reason why a tax is not productive to the public exchequer in proportion to its ratio; and why it has become a sort of apothegm that two and two do not make four in the arithmetic of finance.[137]
—Jean-Baptiste Say, A Treatise on Political Economy, 1851

Real Total State & Local Government Receipts under Kennedy, Reagan and Obama
(annual, Kennedy: 1957-1967, Reagan: 1978-1988, Obama: 2005-2015, deflated with GDP price index to 1970$ and indexed to 100 at NBER cycle troughs in 1961, 1982 and 2009)

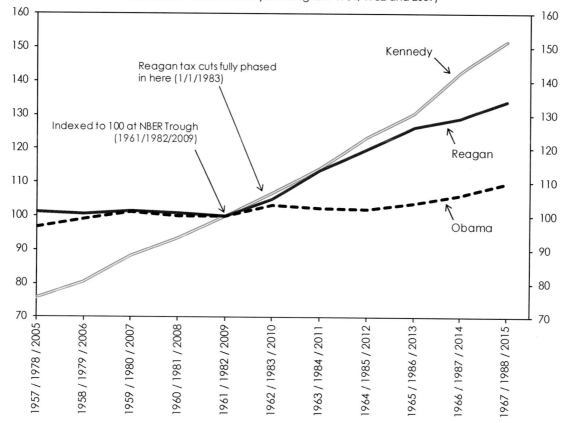

Source: NBER, BEA, Laffer Associates

GDP growth is very powerful in improving the lives of all classes of citizens. Looking back at page 10 and the different rates of economic growth under Presidents Reagan and Obama, this chart demonstrates the impact of those growth differences in the coffers of state and local governments, which in turn allows states to fund the safety net for its residents. Again, supply-side economics explained how lower federal tax rates expand the economic pie and, in this case, unambiguously creates prosperity for state and local economies and their governments.

---

[137] Bruce Bartlett, "Supply-Side Economics: 'Voodoo Economics' or Lasting Contribution?" Laffer Associates, November 11, 2003.

The chart previous page compares and contrasts the effects President Reagan and President Kennedy's tax cuts had on state and local fiscal solvency by way of tax revenues to the effects President Obama's spending, regulation and tax increases had on state and local fiscal solvency. It's eye-opening. What was true for President Reagan was equally true for President Kennedy. The Kennedy and Reagan tax cuts and the ensuing prosperity caused a surge in state and local tax revenues.

If state and local government receipts had grown under President Obama at the rate they grew under President Reagan, 2016 state and local receipts would be $2,906 billion instead of $2,325 billion, or $581 billion (25%) greater. For a related chart, see "States' Rights and States' Wrongs" on the next page.

The 1980 annual report signals the start of a new era of economic thinking. The past has been dominated by economists who focused almost exclusively on the demand side of the economy and who, as a result, were trapped into believing that there is an inevitable trade-off between unemployment and inflation...The Committee's 1980 report says that steady economic growth, created by productivity gains and accompanied by a stable fiscal policy and a gradual reduction in the growth of the money supply over a period of years, can reduce inflation significantly during the 1980's without increasing unemployment. To achieve this goal, the Committee recommends a comprehensive set of policies designed to enhance the productive side, the supply side of the economy.
—Joint Economic Committee, Chairman Lloyd Bentsen (D-TX), 1980

States' Rights and States' Wrongs
When the Going Gets Tough, the States Go Taxing

Liberty produces excessive taxes; the effect of excessive taxes is slavery; and slavery produces a diminution of tribute.[138]
— *Montesquieu, The Spirit of the Laws, 1748*

Net State Legislated Tax Rate Changes as a % of Previous Year Tax Collections
(calendar year changes to take effect the following fiscal year)

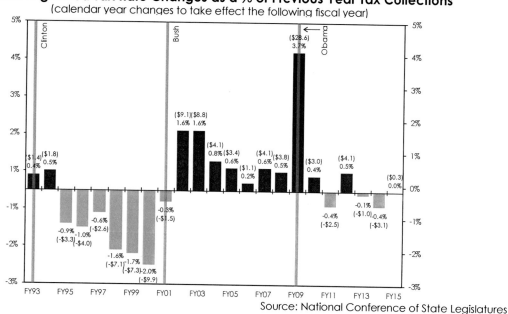

Source: National Conference of State Legislatures

The above chart is a composite of all state "tax rate" increases (red) and decreases (green). These measures are the equivalent of a static revenue increase or decrease i.e. what would revenue have been with a specific tax change if there were no supply-side responses.

Under the Clinton prosperity, states lowered tax rates a lot and because of a strong U.S. economy and supply-side responses states were also fiscally solvent. Under Presidents George W. Bush and Barack Obama, prosperity eluded America and despair was the order of the day. State budgets were put under intense pressure, and desperate state politicians resorted to anti-growth tax increases. For a related chart, see "What If? States and Cities in 2015 Would Have Had $581 Billion More in Their Coffers" on the previous page.

One of the great secrets of American success is that the U.S. is a federation of quasi-independent states with their own jurisdiction over many facets of governance. Competition has created a far more perfect union and has allowed America to become the country it could have been.

My personal observation is that as you go through the process of permanent tax reduction, that there is an awfully good argument to be made for the fact that the revenues of the Government actually increase at a given time. I think it has been proven in previous circumstances. I have no problem in following that sort of thing.
— *Bert Lance, Director of OMB under Jimmy Carter, 1977*

[138] Bruce Bartlett, "Supply-Side Economics: 'Voodoo Economics' or Lasting Contribution?" Laffer Associates, November 11, 2003.

Taxes Redistribute People, Not Income—Richard Vedder
Vis Medicatrix Naturae

To paraphrase Voltaire, *Economists are people who prescribe economic policies of which they know little to cure economic maladies of which they know even less for economies of which they know nothing.*

If ever anyone questioned the power of income taxes in impeding economic growth, these tables should set them straight. Looking at ten-year periods for population growth, payroll growth, personal income growth, gross state product growth, and, yes, even state and local tax revenue growth, those states with no earned income tax have radically outperformed the same number of the highest earned income tax rate states every single decade of the past three decades and earlier.

Nine Zero Earned Income Tax vs. Nine Highest Earned Income Tax (PIT) Rate States

State	As of 1/1/2016	10-Yr. Growth				9-Yr. Growth
		2005-2015			2004-2014	2004-2013
	Top Marginal PIT Rate†	Population	Nonfarm Payroll Employment	Personal Income	Gross State Product‡	State & Local Tax Revenue§
Avg. of 9 Zero Earned Income Tax Rate States*	0.00%	12.9%	8.7%	50.1%	50.8%	57.3%
50-State Avg.*	5.74%	8.8%	5.6%	44.4%	41.2%	44.0%
Avg. of 9 Highest Earned Income Tax Rate States*	10.09%	6.6%	3.7%	43.2%	39.3%	49.9%

* Averages are equal-weighted. † Top Marginal PIT Rate is the top marginal rate on personal earned income imposed as of 1/1/2015 using the tax rate of each state's largest city as a proxy for the local tax. The deductibility of federal taxes from state tax liability is included where applicable. ‡ Gross State Product growth data are 2004 to 2014 because of data release lag. § State & Local Tax Revenue is the growth in state and local tax revenue from the Census Bureau's State & Local Government Finances survey. Because the U.S. Census Bureau did not release state & local finance data for 2003 and due to data release lag, these data are 2004 to 2013. ‖ New Hampshire and Tennessee tax interest and dividend income—so-called "unearned" income—but not ordinary wage income.

Source: Laffer Associates, U.S. Census Bureau, Bureau of Labor Statistics, Bureau of Economic Analysis

Again looking at population growth and real personal income growth, those zero earned income tax states have outperformed the equivalent number of the highest earned income tax rate states using a ten-year moving average of population and personal income growth every single year for the past 42 years, EVERY YEAR!

Ten-year Population Growth for Zero Earned Income Tax States and Highest Income Tax Rate States
(annual, 1970-2015)

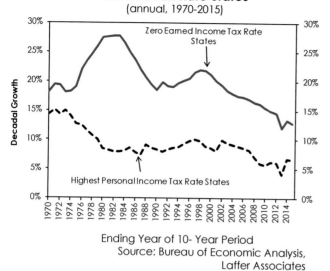

Ending Year of 10- Year Period
Source: Bureau of Economic Analysis,
Laffer Associates

Ten-year Personal Income Growth for Zero Earned Income Tax States and Highest Income Tax Rate States
(annual, 1970-2012)

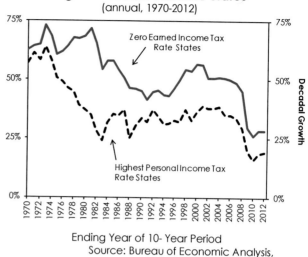

Ending Year of 10- Year Period
Source: Bureau of Economic Analysis,
Laffer Associates

If duties are too high, they lessen the consumption—the collection is eluded and the product to the treasury is not so great as when they are confined within proper and moderate bounds.
— Alexander Hamilton, The Federalist

Nightmare on Elm Street

The people who are trying to make the world worse aren't taking a day off. How can I?
—*Bob Marley, December 1976*

Since 1960, there have been 11 states that have adopted a state income tax. This is their story.

Every single state that adopted an income tax from 1960 to the present has declined as a share of the rest of the nation in every single metric from population and gross state product to state and local tax revenues. Likewise every single one of those 11 states has been in the bottom half of all states in growth of population and gross state product over the past 50 years.

2015 Metrics of the 11 States that Adopted an Income Tax post -1960 versus the 39 Remaining States*

States	First Year of State Income Tax	Maximum State Income Tax Rate*		% Change in Ratio from First Year of State Income Tax to Rest of Nation (Shares of 39 Remaining States)		
		Initial	Current	2015 Population	2015 GSP	2013 State & Local Tax Revenue
Connecticut	1991	1.50 %	6.99 %	-20 %	-21 %	-4 %
New Jersey	1976	2.50	9.97	-27	-23	-5
Ohio	1972	3.50	7.50	-38	-45	-26
Rhode Island	1971	5.25	5.99	-36	-34	-24
Pennsylvania	1971	2.30	6.98	-39	-41	-30
Maine	1969	6.00	7.15	-27	-30	-3
Illinois	1969	2.50	3.75	-36	-42	-19
Nebraska	1968	2.60	6.84	-31	-20	-15
Michigan	1967	2.00	6.65	-37	-57	-49
Indiana	1963	2.00	5.07	-30	-36	-33
West Virginia	1961	5.40	6.50	-52	-54	-39

* Maximum tax rate is top combined state and local tax rate in each state

Sources: Bureau of Economic Analysis, U.S. Census Bureau and ALEC's 2016 Edition of *Rich States Poor States*

Note that the table to the right includes the maximum state and local income tax rate; therefore, the stated rate for Michigan differs from the rate on page 78, which is the state rate.

> *When, on the contrary, I show, a little elaborately, as in the ensuing chapter, that to create wealth will increase the national income and that a large proportion of any increase in the national income will accrue to an Exchequer, amongst whose largest outgoings is the payment of incomes to those who are unemployed and whose receipts are a proportion of the incomes of those who are occupied, I hope the reader will feel, whether or not he thinks himself competent to criticize the argument in detail, that the answer is just what he would expect—that it agrees with the instinctive promptings of his common sense.[139]*
> — *John Maynard Keynes, The Means to Prosperity, 1933*

50-Year Population Growth by State: Annualized Percent Change 1965 to 2015*

50-Year Gross State Product (GSP) Growth by State: Annualized Percent Change 1965 to 2015*

(Orange: 11 states that adopted income tax from 1960 to present, ranked highest to lowest)

Rank	State	% Change
1	Nevada	3.82 %
2	Arizona	2.97
3	Florida	2.48
4	Utah	2.23
5	Colorado	2.04
6	Alaska	2.03
7	Texas	1.97
8	Washington	1.78
9	Idaho	1.78
10	Georgia	1.73
11	California	1.50
12	Oregon	1.48
13	North Carolina	1.46
14	New Mexico	1.46
15	Hawaii	1.43
16	New Hampshire	1.36
17	South Carolina	1.36
18	Virginia	1.29
19	Delaware	1.26
20	Wyoming	1.14
21	Tennessee	1.11
22	Maryland	1.03
23	Oklahoma	0.95
24	Arkansas	0.91
25	Vermont	0.88

Rank	State	% Change
26	Minnesota	0.85 %
27	Montana	0.76
28	Alabama	0.69
29	Kentucky	0.69
30	Wisconsin	0.62
31	Missouri	0.62
32	Indiana	0.59
33	Louisiana	0.58
34	Maine	0.58
35	Mississippi	0.58
36	New Jersey	0.56
37	Kansas	0.56
38	Nebraska	0.51
39	Connecticut	0.46
40	South Dakota	0.43
41	Massachusetts	0.42
42	Illinois	0.37
43	Michigan	0.34
44	Rhode Island	0.34
45	North Dakota	0.31
46	Iowa	0.26
47	Ohio	0.26
48	New York	0.22
49	Pennsylvania	0.19
50	West Virginia	0.06

Source: U.S. Census Bureau

Rank	State	% Change
1	Nevada	8.85 %
2	Arizona	8.45
3	Florida	8.16
4	Colorado	8.03
5	Texas	8.00
6	Utah	7.95
7	Georgia	7.63
8	Alaska	7.57
9	New Hampshire	7.49
10	Washington	7.43
11	Virginia	7.38
12	North Carolina	7.33
13	Oregon	7.18
14	South Carolina	7.18
15	California	7.14
16	North Dakota	7.04
17	Idaho	7.02
18	Maryland	7.02
19	Delaware	7.00
20	Tennessee	6.97
21	Hawaii	6.89
22	New Mexico	6.88
23	Arkansas	6.87
24	Minnesota	6.79
25	Wyoming	6.79

Rank	State	% Change
26	South Dakota	6.77 %
27	Oklahoma	6.73
28	Vermont	6.66
29	Nebraska	6.56
30	Massachusetts	6.55
31	Alabama	6.44
32	Connecticut	6.43
33	Mississippi	6.35
34	Kansas	6.34
35	New Jersey	6.31
36	Louisiana	6.30
37	Montana	6.29
38	Wisconsin	6.25
39	Kentucky	6.22
40	Maine	6.19
41	Iowa	6.06
42	Missouri	6.04
43	Indiana	5.97
44	Rhode Island	5.96
45	New York	5.94
46	Pennsylvania	5.83
47	Illinois	5.81
48	Ohio	5.64
49	West Virginia	5.44
50	Michigan	5.20

Source: Bureau of Economic Analysis

[139] John Maynard Keynes, "Keynes and the Laffer Curve," Adam Smith Institute, January 4, 2011. https://www.adamsmith.org/blog/tax-spending/keynes-and-the-laffer-curve

Progress Comes One Step at a Time, But Over Time, Progress Can Change the World

States With Estate/Inheritance Taxes Over Time

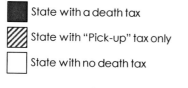

- State with a death tax
- State with "Pick-up" tax only
- State with no death tax

January 1, 1976

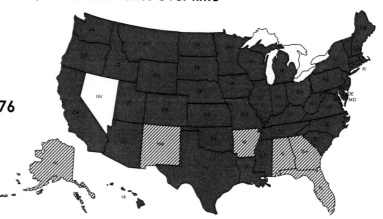

Even California passed Propositions 5 and 6, which repealed the Inheritance and Gift Tax Laws by a vote of 61.8% to 38.2% and 64.4% to 35.6%, respectively, in 1982.

You ought to be able to leave your land and the bulk of your fortune to your children and not the government.
—Hillary Clinton, Fall 2000, while campaigning for Senate in New York

January 1, 2016

Ultimately, the goal of egalitarianism should not be to bring the wealthy down, but to raise the poor up. The estate tax is an impediment to that goal. Ironically, it does more to keep the poor down than to bring down the wealthy. It does not promote equality, but does impose a heavy cost on the economy and society. It should be abolished.
— Bruce Bartlett, 2000

States With Estate Taxes as of 2016		
Connecticut	Maine	New York
Delaware	Maryland	Oregon
Hawaii	Massachusetts	Pennsylvania
Illinois	Minnesota	Rhode Island
Iowa	Nebraska	Vermont
Kentucky	New Jersey	Washington

There has been a consistent, longstanding, grassroots groundswell at the state level to eliminate the inheritance and estate tax. In 1976, for example, there was only one state (Nevada) without an inheritance or estate tax. Six states at that time had only a "pick-up" tax to offset the federal tax credit. 43 states in 1976 had either an inheritance or estate tax, or both. Since 1976, there has been a literal rush to the exit and, as of today, there are 32 states without gift, estate or inheritance taxes, and there are more to come. Grandpa can finally feel at ease to pass on to the hereafter.

A Victory: The Death of the Inventory Tax
States With Inventory Taxes Over Time

All taxes upon the transference of property of every kind, so far as they diminish the capital value of that property, tend to diminish the funds destined for the maintenance of productive labor.[140]
—Adam Smith, *Wealth of Nations*

If there are two locations, A and B, and taxes are raised in B and lowered in A, producers, manufactures and people will move from B to A.

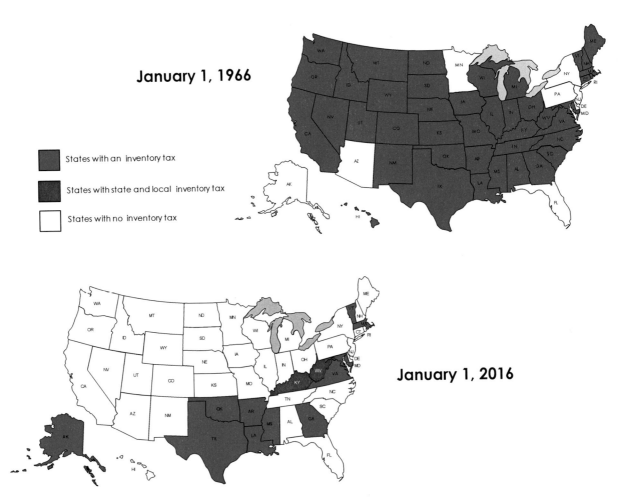

January 1, 1966

States with an inventory tax

States with state and local inventory tax

States with no inventory tax

January 1, 2016

One of the most prominent taxes over the years has been the inventory tax. In most states, the inventory tax was assessed on inventories in the state as of midnight on December 31st. Prior to California's elimination of its inventory tax, trucks used to line up for miles and miles on all the major freeways entering California on December 31st, waiting for the stroke of midnight to enter

---

[140] Bruce Bartlett, "Wealth, Mobility, Inheritance and the Estate Tax," Laffer Associates, June 6, 2000.

the state without having to pay that year's inventory tax. Economics is all about incentives.

Arthur Laffer was one of three sponsors (along with Howard Jarvis) of a California state initiative, Proposition 9, which would have eliminated the state's inventory tax. That initiative failed at the ballot box, but only a few months later, Governor Brown successfully eliminated the inventory tax legislatively.

Today, there are only two states with both state and local inventory taxes—West Virginia and Kentucky (in red for 2016)—the other states that have inventory taxes have those taxes only at the local level (in blue for 2016).

"A beautiful theory, killed by a nasty, ugly little fact"—Thomas Huxley

Right-to-Work States Grow Faster

There are few policies more conducive to economic growth than the adoption of Right-to-Work legislation. It's been a long journey, from the days of Walter Reuther, John L. Lewis and Jimmy Hoffa through the showdowns with the Air Traffic Controllers, on to today, but what a journey it's been. And there's more to come.

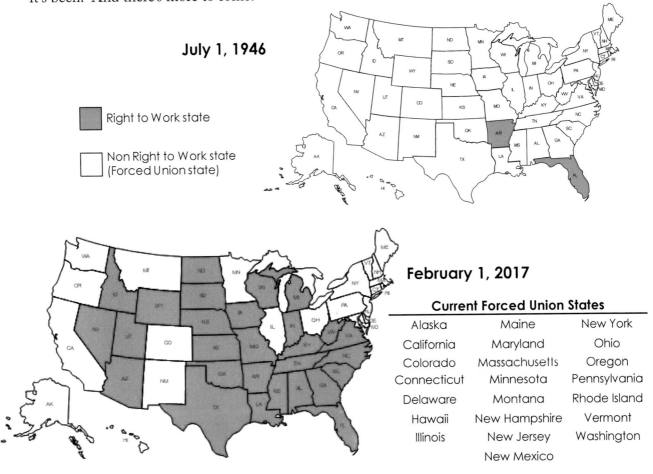

July 1, 1946

■ Right to Work state

☐ Non Right to Work state
(Forced Union state)

February 1, 2017

Current Forced Union States

Alaska	Maine	New York
California	Maryland	Ohio
Colorado	Massachusetts	Oregon
Connecticut	Minnesota	Pennsylvania
Delaware	Montana	Rhode Island
Hawaii	New Hampshire	Vermont
Illinois	New Jersey	Washington
	New Mexico	

Economic Performance: 22 Right-to-Work States vs. 28 Forced-Union States
(performance metrics are 10-year % change from 2004-2014 unless otherwise indicated)

State	1/1/2012 RTW? Yes=1**	2004-2014 Population	2005-2014 Net Domestic In-Migration†	2004-2014 Nonfarm Payroll Employment	2004-2014 Personal Income	2004-2014 Gross State Product	2002-2012 State & Local Tax Revenue‡
Avg. of 22 Right-to-Work States*	1.00	12.40%	3.06%	9.06%	54.74%	50.65%	65.64%
50-State Avg.*	0.44	8.84%	0.71%	6.14%	48.42%	43.59%	63.00%
Avg. of 28 Forced-Union States*	0.00	6.04%	-1.14%	3.86%	43.46%	38.04%	60.93%

* Equal-weighted averages
** RTW status is as of 1/1/2012. Since that date, Indiana, Michigan, Wisconsin, Kentucky, West Virginia and Missouri have passed RTW laws. We did not include these six states in the table above because they have only been RTW for a very brief portion of the analysis period.
† Net domestic migration is calculated as the ten-year (2005-2014) sum of net domestic in-migrants divided by the mid-year (2010) population.
‡ 2002-2012 due to Census Bureau data release lag.
Source: Laffer Associates, U.S. Census Bureau, Bureau of Labor Statistics, Bureau of Economic Analysis

Superman, Wyatt Earp and Dorothy: The Story of Kansas

We join the story of Kansas in January 2011, when former U.S. Senator Sam Brownback takes office as Kansas' 46th Governor along with a Republican-controlled House (92 Rs and 33 Ds) and Senate (32 Rs and 8 Ds). The Kansas economy, while far from being a catastrophe, had been underperforming for a long time. The unemployment rate was 6.8%. Using IRS data of tax filers, in every single year from TY1992 through TY2012, Kansas has experienced a net loss of Adjusted Gross Income (AGI) to the rest of the nation. If, over the past 21 years before Gov. Brownback's tax cuts took effect, the net flow of AGI had been zero instead of what it actually was, the state of Kansas would now have almost $4 billion of additional AGI per year and all the derivative benefits that come with higher incomes. And perhaps worst of all, Kansas' pension system was ranked second worst in the nation in terms of solvency, with a funding ratio in the 50% range.

To propel the Kansas economy into prosperity, Gov. Brownback's proposed economic agenda would have reduced the highest income tax rate to 4.9% from 6.45% and all other income tax rates to 3%. He also proposed expanding standard deductions from $4,500 to $9,000 and exempting non-wage pass-through income (excluding capital gains, interest and dividends) reported by Partnerships, LLCs, LLPs, "S"-corporations and sole proprietorships from state INCOME taxes. Down the road, Gov. Brownback's intentions included further pro-growth tax rate cuts.

To "pay" for these proposed tax changes, Gov. Brownback also proposed keeping the 1% state sales tax increase that was set to expire and eliminating many tax credits and deductions, including the mortgage interest deduction, the earned income tax credit and the child tax credit. All in, Brownback's proposed legislation was scored as a tax cut of less than $90 million, which given total FY 2011 tax revenues of $5,693 million is far from "a radical tax cut." But for Gov. Brownback, nothing was as easy as it seemed.

The day Gov. Brownback took office, he was confronted by anti-Brownback Senators, many from his own party who delayed, deferred and obstructed his tax plan. As a final gesture of defiance, the Senate rushed passage of a substitute for House Bill 2117 on May 22nd, 2012, which stripped Gov. Brownback's bill of all of the "pay for" items to finance the income tax cut. The Senate bill was projected to initially cost over $230 million versus Gov. Brownback's proposal of $90 million, with that difference increasing in the out years. The Senate bill took precedence over the House bill, which had been passed some 15 minutes after the Senate bill was passed.

The anti-Brownback Senators expected Gov. Brownback to cower and then veto the Senate bill, thus giving up on his dream of a Kansas recovery. They were wrong; Gov. Brownback signed the Senate bill. But, just for the record, the budgetary costs of the actual bill compared to the bill the Governor had originally proposed had been increased by $140 million. Had the Governor's proposal taken effect at the beginning of his term—i.e. two years before it actually took effect—the story of Kansas growth would be much different.

In righteous indignation, allies of Governor Brownback sought retribution from the anti-Brownback Senators, and they got it. Eight incumbent Republican Senators were denied re-nomination in the Republican primary held on August 7th, 2012 including the anti-Brownback ringleader and Senate President Stephen Morris. Four open Senate seats in that primary were also captured by Brownback supporters and this episode of the anti-Brownback insurrection was dead in its tracks.

After the general election in November 2012, the composition of the Kansas legislature was completely revamped even though ostensibly the Republican Senate majority was little changed, 31/9 versus 32/8. But more was to come.

Concurrent with the political fireworks, unrelated budget forces were also in the works, causing shortfalls in revenues. Many political opponents have been quick to lay blame on the Kansas tax plan, but there are several reasons why this could not be further from the truth:

Every single year for the ten years, from FY2003 through FY2012, the legislature had suspended the requirement that the state have 7½% of total annual budget expenditures as an ending cash balance, but not for FY2013 or FY2014. Requiring higher ending cash balances alone absorbed some $200 to $500 million of funds. To respond to a state Supreme Court ruling, budget outlays for schools were increased by $65 million annually for FY2014 and FY2015. Additional funds—in the vicinity of $400 million—were also necessitated to reduce the substantial underfunding of state employee pensions. In fact, Kansas' needs were sufficiently great that they bonded some $1 billion to tide the state over and increased employer and employee contributions.

In addition, there was a serious FY2014 tax revenue overestimate resulting from overestimating increases in Kansas' personal unearned income. President Obama had allowed the Bush tax cuts to expire January 1, 2013 on all sorts of unearned income, including dividends and capital gains. Anticipating these tax changes, investors and businesses accelerated realizations of capital gains and payments of dividends into calendar year 2012 from calendar year 2013. Thus, there was an abnormal, but easily explainable, surge in federal tax revenues in calendar year 2012 and a more substantial drop-off in calendar year 2013.

For Kansas (and many other states), the surge in capital gains and dividends in calendar year 2012 came as a surprise and resulted in a surge in tax revenues for FY2013. As most states do, future tax revenue projections in Kansas are basically extrapolations of past changes, so Kansas not only missed the retrenchment of revenues in 2014, but also incorrectly projected large increases for 2014. In TY2012, for example, the Standard & Poor's rose 13% and capital gains income in Kansas grew 47.7%. In TY2013, the Standard & Poor's gained 30%, but Kansas capital gains income fell by 19.2%. In all, the forecast error left a shortfall from the state's budget of some $300 million.

A reporting error from the Kansas Department of Finance had it that in 2012 there were 180,000 pass-through entities whose taxes were reduced to zero and in 2014 this number increases to 330,000 resulting in a $50 million underestimate of tax receipts. Governor Brownback critics hailed this as a give-away to the rich causing all sorts of regular businesses to file as pass-throughs. In point of fact, when proposed, the number of pass-through entities was 330,000, the number actually filed was 339,000.

Additionally, discrepancy between projected revenue and actual revenue can be largely attributed to the rural recession that most of Western Kansas experienced. Because of national headwinds, oil prices dropped precipitously, with crop prices dropping 40-60%, and cattle prices dropping 23%. With farmers and ranchers receiving far less for their crops and cattle, they in turn aren't purchasing new equipment, making upgrades, or hiring new farm hands.

And lastly, if you look at the numbers, we can quickly identify the prime culprits of the revenue shortfall—corporate taxes, which weren't touched in the Kansas tax plan, were down in Kansas as they are nationally and sales tax revenues, which the legislature raised, were down as well. Yet, individual income taxes, which were cut, were _up_.

While the fact is that Kansas had a large negative shock to its overall budget in 2014 and 2015, the underlying causes were only peripherally related to Brownback's tax bill. But such a shortfall always causes an uproar: warnings of school closures, fears of lessened police protection and threatened lack of funds for the needy. 2014 being an election year, the normal hype was greatly magnified by 1.) the disgruntled anti-Brownback former Senators who had been thrown out of office and now sided with Brownback's Democratic challenger, 2.) a vulnerable Senator Pat Roberts running for reelection and 3.) the reelection campaign for Governor Brownback himself. It was the perfect storm, attracting nationwide attention, including numerous editorials even from *The New York Times* and N.P.R., no less.

The truth of the matter is that, according to the U.S. Census Bureau, the number of Missourians moving to Kansas tripled after Gov. Brownback's tax cuts. According to the IRS, Kansas reversed 19 years of financial losses to Missouri in the first year of the tax plan alone, with further gains in 2014; according to the U.S. Labor Department, Kansas had a near record number of private sector jobs following the tax cuts; and according to the Department of Revenue, during the first two years of the tax plan alone, 18,000 brand new small businesses sprouted up under the pro-growth tax plan.

Therefore, in November 2014, in spite of all the national backlash, Gov. Brownback was easily re-nominated and reelected, along with U.S. Senator Pat Roberts. After the elections, the Kansas House and Senate were even more Republican than they had been when Brownback took office, with 97 Rs to 28 Ds and 32 Rs to 8 Ds, respectively—hardly a wholesale repudiation of Brownback, his slate of legislators or supply-side economics. Apparently, the electorate really doesn't want to balance the state's budget by unbalancing the budgets of everyday Kansans.

Kansas is back, Toto. As of March 2016, Kansas' unemployment rate is 3.9%, the 11th lowest in the nation. Kansas' private sector employment is growing faster since the tax cuts took effect than all of its neighbors, save for steroidal Colorado. Kansas City, Kansas is adding more private sector jobs than is Kansas City, Missouri. Income taxes for individuals, families and small businesses have been reduced by 30%. Kansas' pension funding is now 22nd best in the nation—a vast improvement from the state's second-worst in the nation ranking back when Governor Brownback took office. The pension system's funding ratio is now 62% and projected to soon rise to 66%—considered well into the "safe zone" as far as funding ratios go. And, lastly, Superman, Wyatt Earp and Dorothy are cheering like mad in heaven.

And one observation appears very much in order. Because of Gov. Brownback's policies, the legislature in Missouri passed a 10% income tax rate cut, which the less than enlightened Missouri Governor Jay Nixon quickly vetoed. But not to be put off, Missouri's legislature then passed the tax cut over the Governor's veto. Imitation is the sincerest form of flattery. Just wait and see what happens when these pro-growth policies have had sufficient time to have their full supply-side effects materialize.

Superman   Wyatt Earp   Dorothy and Toto

A Few Great Residents of Kansas

Who Says You Can't Have Low Taxes, Great Services and Fiscal Soundness? NOT Tennessee

Tennessee Taxes
(Taxes: FY13-14, GSP: 2014, Ranking:
lowest tax burden = 1, highest tax burden = 50)

- Tennessee has no earned income tax.

- Tennessee has eliminated its gift and estate tax (2016).

- Tennessee is phasing out its unearned income tax (2022).

- Tennessee has the 9th lowest property tax.

- Tennessee has the 3rd lowest total tax burden of all U.S. states.

	Tennessee	U.S. Rank
Earned Income Tax	0%	1
Unearned Income Tax*	0%	1
Estate and Gift Tax	0%	1
Property Tax as % of GSP	1.8%	9
Corporate Tax as % of GSP	0.4%	38
Sales Tax as % of GSP	3.8%	41
All Other Tax as % of GSP	0.8%	6
Total Tax Burden	6.8%	3

* The Hall Tax is currently in the process of being phased out and will be eliminated as of 2022. Source: ALEC Rich States Poor States, Bureau of Economic Analysis, Census Bureau

Outcomes Matter:

- Tennessee has a $2 billion surplus (out of a $35 billion budget in 2016).[141]

- Tennessee's credit rating (2016) is tied for 1st in the nation: AAA from all three of the major credit rating agencies.[142]

- Tennessee's state and local government employee pensions are 5th best funded (98.8% in 2014).

- Tennessee controls costs by paying Full-Time Equivalent Employees (FTEE) 8th lowest (in 2015).[143]

- Tennessee also has the 14th least number of FTEEs per 10,000 population in 2015.

- Tennessee had the largest increase in employment-to-population in the nation from Nov. 2015 to Nov. 2016 (55,600 additional jobs, or 2.2% of its population).

- From 2005-2016, Tennessee has witnessed the nation's 9th largest percentage increase in net in-migration as a share of population of any state in the nation (334,000 people).

- From 2005-2014, Tennessee had the nation's 12th greatest net inflow of Adjusted Gross Income (4.5% of total AGI).

- Tennessee highways are 18th best in the nation, versus 37th best in 1987.

[141] Tom Humphrey, "Tenn. Legislators talk tax cuts in light of $2B cash surplus," The Tennessean, December 24, 2016. http://www.tennessean.com/story/news/local/2016/12/24/tenn-legislators-talk-tax-cuts-light-2b-cash-surplus/95749390/
[142] Cari Wage Gervin, "State upgraded to AAA bond rating," Nashville Post, May 26, 2016. http://www.nashvillepost.com/business/article/20781279/state-upgraded-to-aaa-bond-rating
[143] Bureau of Labor Statistics.

- As measured by National Association of Education Progress (NAEP), Tennessee's NAEP scores saw the fastest improvement of any state for math and reading among all students tested (4th grade and 8th grade students) in 2013.[144] Notably, growth was very strong for African American students in 2013.[145] And in 2016, Tennessee's science scores improved more than any other state in the nation.

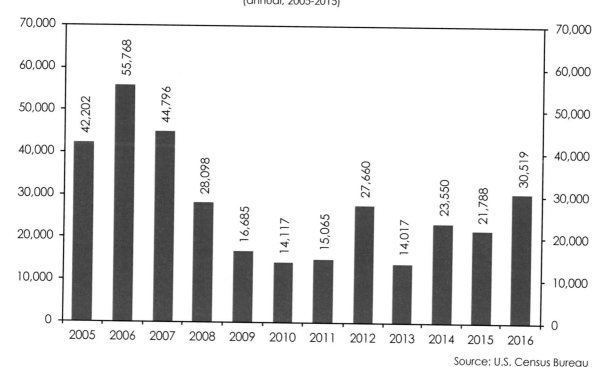

Tennessee Net Domestic Migration
(annual, 2005-2015)

Source: U.S. Census Bureau

[144] According to its website, "The National Assessment of Educational Progress (NAEP) is the largest nationally representative and continuing assessment of what America's students know and can do in various subject areas. Paper-and-pencil assessments are conducted periodically in mathematics, reading, science, writing, the arts, civics, economics, geography, U.S. history, and in Technology and Engineering Literacy (TEL)." Source: "NAEP Overview," National Center for Education Statistics. https://nces.ed.gov/nationsreportcard/about/
[145] "Gov. Haslam: TN is fastest-improving state in education, according to NAEP results," WSMV online, December 5, 2013. http://www.wsmv.com/story/23904415/gov-haslam-expected-to-make-big-education-announcement

West-By God-Virginia

West Virginia Personal Income as a Share of U.S. Personal Income and West Virginia's Tax History
(annual, 1929-2014)

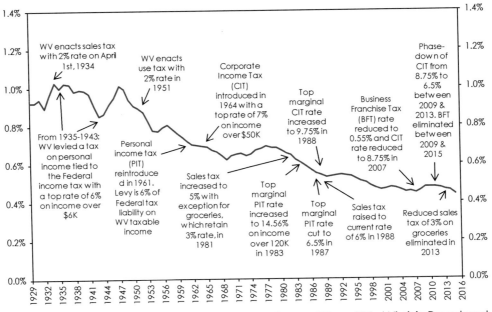

Source: BEA and West Virginia Department of Revenue

Taxes Are a People Repellent
Population Levels Indexed: West Virginia, Select States and the U.S.
(annual, 1977-2014, index 1977 = 100)

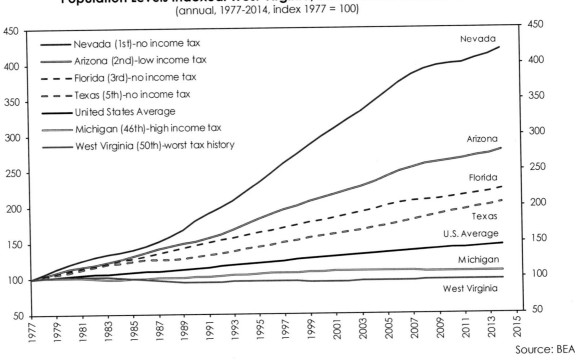

Source: BEA

Kentucky

A Prime Example of Tax Complexity—Kentucky's Property Tax in Louisville, Jefferson County

Consider Louisville-Jefferson County, with its 105 property tax jurisdictions. First, all qualifying inventory in Louisville-Jefferson County is subject to state inventory taxation. At the county level, motor vehicles held for sale, manufacturers' raw materials are exempt from taxation by statute as they are in all local jurisdictions, but manufacturers finished goods and merchants inventory, are subject to taxation at a rate of 98.2 cents per $100 market value. Two school districts operate in Louisville-Jefferson County and both levy taxes on merchant's inventories (at rates of 98.2 cents and 71 cents per $100 of market value)—so long as the inventories are not considered Goods-In-Transit (GIT), which are exempt from city, county and school district taxation. Of the 21 special districts in Louisville-Jefferson County, 19 tax merchant's inventory and 18 tax inventory Goods-In-Transit (GIT) at varying rates (Note that Goods-In-Transit are exempt from all tax jurisdictions except special districts—of which 776 with the authority to tax were active in Kentucky in 2012, making Goods-In-Transit (GIT) subject to taxation across much of Kentucky).[146] Considering that revenues from taxes in these special districts are devoted to provision of ambulance services, fire department services, garbage collection and parks services, and assuming businesses operating in Louisville-Jefferson County have access to most or all of these services, those businesses would be subject to inventory taxes in several special tax jurisdictions. Of the 81 city-level districts that tax inventory in Louisville-Jefferson County, four tax merchant's inventory.

Kentucky taxes tangible personal property at varying rates depending on the type of property. For example, raw materials are taxed at a state rate of $0.05 per $100 valuation and are exempt from local taxation.[147] Manufacturing machinery is taxed at a rate of $0.15 per $100 valuation at the state level and is exempt from taxation at the local level.[148] Business furniture and computer equipment is taxed at a rate of $0.45 per $100 value at the state level and is not exempt from local tangible property tax taxation. According to Kentucky's Cabinet for Economic Development, aggregate local tax rates for tangible property taxes vary, "averaging $0.45 per $100 of assessed market value among the 120 counties [the total number of counties in Kentucky] and $0.2863 per $100 of value in the 299 cities that levy the tax."[149] According to the Kentucky

---

[146] Adam H. Edelen, "Ghost Government: A Report on Special Districts in Kentucky," Commonwealth of Kentucky, Auditor of Public Accounts, 2012. http://apps.auditor.ky.gov/public/theregistry/2012GhostGovernmentSpecialDistrictsReport.pdf
[147] "FactSheet: Kentucky Business Taxes," Cabinet for Economic Development, December 2015. https://www.thinkkentucky.com/kyedc/pdfs/KYBusinessTaxes.pdf
[148] Ibid.
[149] Ibid.

Department of Revenue, the weighted average state and local tangible property tax rate is $0.64 cents per $100 of assessed market value.[150]

Addressing the citizens of Kentucky of his intent to move to Texas, Davey Crockett spoke these memorable words, *"Y'all can go to Hell, I'm going to Texas!"*

North Carolina
The North Carolina Lesson: If you tax people less for working and pay people less for not working, you'll get a boom.

In 2013, North Carolina cut personal and corporate income tax rates, eliminated the death tax, and trimmed unemployment benefits.[151]
- Top income tax rate cut from 7.75% to 5.75%.
- Corporate tax rate down from 6.9% to 5%.
- Estate tax topping out at 16% eliminated.
- Unemployment benefits cut from $535 to $350 per week.
- Unemployment duration was reduced from ~26 weeks to 12 (sliding) and 20 weeks.

A series of funny things happened:
- Jobs growth boomed. There were 200,000 new jobs from 2013-15.
- Unemployment fell to 5.7% from 7.8%.
- The unemployment-insurance fund went from deficit to surplus.
- The budget racked up a surplus as revenues surged by 6%.
- North Carolina's AAA bond rating was upheld on the basis of the "state's long history of conservative fiscal practices, an economy that continues to recover and expand, and declining debt levels."[152]

We guess the old adage is still true: if you tax people who work and pay people who don't work, you'll get a lot of people not working. The converse is also true: tax people less for working and pay them less for not working and you'll have a boom.

Public policy designed to help workers who lost their jobs can lead to structural unemployment as an unintended side effect... The drawback to this generosity is that it reduces the incentive to quickly find a new job, and by keeping more people searching for longer, the benefits increase structural and frictional unemployment.[153]
— Paul Krugman on unemployment compensation in 2010

[150] "2015 Property Tax Handbook," Kentucky Department of Revenue, 2015.
[151] Stephen Moore, "The Tax-Cut Payoff in Carolina," Wall Street Journal, June3, 2015. https://www.wsj.com/articles/the-tax-cut-payoff-in-carolina-1433373095
[152] Rex Sinquefield, "Give North Carolina More Credit For Its AAA Bond Rating" Forbes, February 16, 2016.
[153] http://www.allhallows.org/ourpages/auto/2012/9/7/60346251/Krugmans%20Economics%20for%20AP%20Text%20Book.pdf

Taxes Scare Dollars Away
Arizona, Florida, Nevada, Wyoming vs. Connecticut, Illinois, New York, New Jersey, Ohio

The U.S. Internal Revenue Service (IRS) has provided tax migration data for 22 years reflecting the state where people filed their tax return this year versus last year and their adjusted gross incomes. These data more than anything show how people vote with their feet where taxes are concerned. We chose to track five loser states and four winner states that are not discussed elsewhere in the Template, and just how much income they have lost and gained as a result of state policies.

Net In-AGI as a Percentage of Total AGI Filed in a Given Year vs. Tax Revenues Rank
(annual, AGI: FY9293-1213, three-year aggregates, FY1314-1415, two-year aggregate)

9293 to 9495		9596 to 9798		9899 to 0001		0102 to 0304		0405 to 0607		0708 to 0910		1011 to 1213		1314 to 1415	
NV	3.8%	NV	3.8%	NV	3.2%	NV	3.1%	NV	2.2%	SC	1.4%	FL	1.6%	FL	2.3%
AZ	2.7%	AZ	2.3%	FL	2.0%	FL	2.3%	AZ	2.1%	MT	1.3%	SC	1.4%	NV	2.1%
ID	2.1%	FL	1.9%	AZ	1.9%	AZ	1.7%	FL	2.0%	WY	1.1%	NV	1.3%	SC	1.4%
CO	1.8%	CO	1.3%	CO	1.2%	MT	1.2%	SC	1.8%	FL	1.0%	WY	1.0%	AZ	0.8%
FL	1.8%	NC	1.2%	NH	1.1%	ID	1.1%	ID	1.6%	NC	0.9%	MT	0.9%	WY	0.7%
MT	1.5%	SC	1.1%	ID	1.0%	SC	1.1%	NC	1.3%	AZ	0.8%	ID	0.8%	MT	0.6%
NC	1.3%	ID	1.1%	SC	1.0%	NH	1.0%	MT	1.1%	NV	0.7%	AZ	0.8%	TX	0.6%
NM	1.3%	GA	1.0%	WY	1.0%	ME	1.0%	WY	1.0%	CO	0.7%	CO	0.7%	OR	0.6%
GA	1.3%	OR	0.8%	NC	0.9%	WY	0.9%	OR	0.9%	TX	0.6%	TX	0.7%	CO	0.6%
OR	1.3%	WY	0.8%	ME	0.8%	NC	0.6%	TN	0.9%	SD	0.5%	NC	0.6%	NC	0.5%
AR	1.2%	NH	0.8%	VT	0.7%	DE	0.6%	WA	0.8%	TN	0.5%	ND	0.6%	TN	0.5%
UT	1.1%	WA	0.7%	MT	0.5%	OR	0.5%	CO	0.7%	WA	0.5%	WA	0.5%	WA	0.5%
TN	1.0%	TN	0.6%	GA	0.5%	VT	0.5%	NM	0.7%	OR	0.5%	HI	0.5%	ID	0.5%
WA	0.9%	MT	0.6%	DE	0.3%	HI	0.4%	UT	0.6%	ID	0.4%	OR	0.4%	DE	0.4%
WY	0.8%	VT	0.5%	WA	0.3%	NM	0.4%	AR	0.6%	NM	0.3%	TN	0.4%	HI	0.3%
SC	0.8%	TX	0.4%	TN	0.3%	TN	0.4%	NH	0.6%	UT	0.3%	ME	0.3%	SD	0.3%
VT	0.6%	AR	0.4%	OR	0.2%	AR	0.4%	TX	0.6%	DE	0.3%	SD	0.3%	ND	0.2%
NH	0.6%	ME	0.3%	AR	0.2%	WA	0.3%	GA	0.6%	AL	0.3%	NH	0.2%	UT	0.2%
SD	0.6%	MS	0.3%	TX	0.2%	GA	0.2%	DE	0.5%	AR	0.3%	UT	0.2%	GA	0.1%
MS	0.4%	UT	0.2%	VA	0.2%	VA	0.2%	SD	0.5%	GA	0.3%	DE	0.2%	NH	0.0%
TX	0.4%	AL	0.2%	SD	0.1%	RI	0.2%	AL	0.4%	OK	0.2%	OK	0.1%	ME	0.0%
AL	0.3%	KY	0.0%	RI	0.0%	SD	0.2%	VT	0.3%	WV	0.1%	AL	0.1%	AL	-0.1%
KY	0.2%	DE	0.0%	CA	0.0%	CO	0.2%	ME	0.2%	KY	0.1%	GA	0.0%	CA	-0.1%
DE	0.2%	VA	-0.1%	KY	0.0%	TX	0.1%	KY	0.1%	VT	0.1%	KY	0.0%	AR	-0.1%
WV	0.2%	OK	-0.1%	MS	0.0%	AL	0.1%	HI	0.1%	NH	0.1%	AR	-0.1%	OK	-0.1%
VA	0.2%	MO	-0.1%	WI	-0.1%	WV	0.1%	WV	0.1%	VA	0.0%	CA	-0.1%	MO	-0.2%
WI	0.2%	SD	-0.1%	AL	-0.1%	KY	0.1%	OK	0.0%	MS	0.0%	VT	-0.2%	IN	-0.3%
IN	0.1%	NM	-0.1%	MA	-0.2%	MS	0.1%	MS	0.0%	ME	0.0%	IA	-0.2%	MI	-0.3%
MO	0.1%	IN	-0.2%	MN	-0.2%	WI	0.0%	MO	0.0%	HI	0.0%	IN	-0.2%	KY	-0.3%
MN	0.1%	WI	-0.2%	MO	-0.3%	PA	-0.1%	VA	-0.1%	LA	-0.1%	MS	-0.2%	IA	-0.3%
ME	-0.1%	WV	-0.2%	MD	-0.3%	MO	-0.1%	PA	-0.1%	MO	-0.1%	LA	-0.2%	MA	-0.3%
OK	-0.1%	MA	-0.2%	UT	-0.3%	MD	-0.2%	WI	-0.2%	PA	-0.1%	PA	-0.2%	WV	-0.3%
KS	-0.2%	KS	-0.3%	IN	-0.3%	UT	-0.2%	IN	-0.2%	IA	-0.1%	VA	-0.2%	WI	-0.3%
PA	-0.2%	MN	-0.3%	HI	-0.4%	CT	-0.2%	MN	-0.3%	ND	-0.1%	MO	-0.2%	PA	-0.4%
NE	-0.2%	MI	-0.3%	PA	-0.4%	MN	-0.3%	IA	-0.3%	CA	-0.2%	WV	-0.3%	RI	-0.4%
MD	-0.3%	CA	-0.3%	MI	-0.4%	OK	-0.3%	KS	-0.3%	IN	-0.2%	WI	-0.3%	LA	-0.4%
IA	-0.3%	PA	-0.4%	WV	-0.4%	IN	-0.3%	NE	-0.4%	MA	-0.2%	NE	-0.3%	MS	-0.4%
OH	-0.3%	OH	-0.4%	CT	-0.5%	MI	-0.4%	CT	-0.5%	MN	-0.2%	MI	-0.3%	VA	-0.4%
MI	-0.3%	IA	-0.5%	OK	-0.5%	CA	-0.4%	AK	-0.5%	WI	-0.3%	NM	-0.3%	OH	-0.4%
LA	-0.4%	NE	-0.5%	NJ	-0.6%	LA	-0.4%	ND	-0.6%	KS	-0.3%	MN	-0.3%	MN	-0.4%
MA	-0.4%	MD	-0.5%	NM	-0.6%	IA	-0.5%	MD	-0.6%	NE	-0.3%	MA	-0.4%	NE	-0.4%
NJ	-0.5%	LA	-0.5%	OH	-0.6%	NE	-0.5%	CA	-0.6%	MD	-0.3%	KS	-0.4%	KS	-0.5%
ND	-0.6%	NJ	-0.6%	KS	-0.7%	OH	-0.5%	IL	-0.6%	AK	-0.4%	OH	-0.5%	VT	-0.5%
CT	-0.6%	RI	-0.6%	IA	-0.7%	AK	-0.5%	OH	-0.7%	DC	-0.4%	RI	-0.5%	NM	-0.5%
IL	-0.6%	CT	-0.7%	LA	-0.8%	KS	-0.5%	MI	-0.8%	CT	-0.4%	MD	-0.5%	MD	-0.6%
HI	-0.7%	IL	-0.8%	IL	-0.8%	OH	-0.5%	NJ	-0.8%	IL	-0.5%	NJ	-0.6%	NY	-0.7%
RI	-1.1%	ND	-0.8%	NE	-0.9%	MA	-0.7%	MA	-0.8%	NJ	-0.5%	NY	-0.7%	CT	-0.8%
CA	-1.2%	HI	-1.0%	NY	-0.9%	IL	-0.7%	RI	-0.9%	OH	-0.6%	IL	-0.8%	NJ	-0.9%
AK	-1.2%	AK	-1.1%	DC	-1.1%	ND	-0.8%	NY	-1.2%	RI	-0.7%	CT	-1.0%	AK	-0.9%
NY	-1.3%	NY	-1.3%	AK	-1.2%	NY	-1.0%	DC	-1.2%	NY	-0.7%	AK	-1.3%	IL	-1.0%
DC	-4.0%	DC	-3.3%	ND	-1.3%	DC	-2.0%	LA	-1.4%	MI	-0.9%	DC	-1.5%	DC	-1.1%

It was Grace that taught my heart to fear and Grace my fear relieved.
—John Newton, "Amazing Grace"

Down and Out in the Motor City

According to Larry Gatlin, the definition of bankruptcy is *"When your outgo exceeds your income, your upkeep will be your downfall."*

Detroit fits that definition. But the origins of Detroit's bankruptcy are far from unique or exclusively Detroit's fault. And while Detroit's corruption-ridden city government and unfunded pension fund liabilities are the proximate cause of Detroit's bankruptcy, the root causes are far deeper.

Who could ever have imagined a day when Michigan, the home of the United Auto Workers union and the Teamsters, would become a right-to-work state? Or who could have ever imagined the bankruptcy of Detroit, which in 1950 had a population of 1.8 million mostly prosperous people, and was the nation's 5th largest city? In 2016, Detroit had only 680,000 mostly poor people, pushing it down to the nation's 21st largest city, and had one of the highest violent crime rates in the nation—Detroit ranked first in the nation for violent crime in 2014, but ranked second in 2015. Detroit's police personnel per 10,000 of population was also the lowest in the nation.

Detroit is also a part of Michigan, which over the decade of 2005 through 2015, had had the lowest population growth, bar none, in all 50 states; 1.3% versus the U.S. average of 8.8%. Michigan's labor force growth, employment growth, gross state product growth, state and local tax revenue growth are also all the very lowest in the nation, with income per capita and productivity growth very low as well. Yikes!

Michigan Economic Metrics (2005-2015)

Categories	U.S. Rank #1 Best, 50 Worst	Actual Decade % Change
Labor force growth (2005-2015)	50th	-6.68%
Employment growth (2005-2015)	50th	-3.33%
Gross state product growth (2005-2015)	50th	17.73%
State and local tax revenue growth (2004-2013)	50th	10.88%
Income per capita growth (2005-2015)	43rd	28.90%
Productivity growth (2005-2015)	42nd	24.18%

In 2016, Michigan had a state income tax of 4.25% and a corporate tax rate of 6%.

- The federal 35% corporate rate, especially when compared to the average of the OECD if 22.8%, has hurt Michigan's automotive industry, which faces competitors from all over the world.
- Michigan is 3rd-lowest in the nation in per-capita government services.
- But Michigan pays state employees 5% above the national average and has exceptionally generous retirement and health benefits.

In 1967, under Governor Romney's leadership, Michigan initiated a state income tax, initially setting the highest rate at 2.6% using federal Adjusted Gross Income (AGI) as its tax base. The state's income tax rate peaked in 1983 at 6.35% and is now down to 4.25%.

Even though a 4.25% maximum tax rate is a lot better than a 6.35% tax rate, those high historical tax rates have surely damaged Michigan's economy. A 6.35% personal income tax rate surely drives people away, but a 4.25% tax rate won't lure them back. The state's corporate tax rate as of 2016 stands at 6%. The city of Detroit also has its own income tax of 2.4% and a corporate tax of 2%.

These unwarranted burdensome taxes on business have added to Detroit's and Michigan's decline. Again, there's no real solution for Detroit that doesn't include tax reform in Michigan.

See "Detroit" on last page.

The ill-conceived economic policies and real leadership vacuum, locally and at the state level, set the stage for Detroit's failure, ultimately bringing this iconic American city to its knees. If it can happen in Detroit, we now ask, what other U.S. cities may be facing the same fiscal disaster? Chicago? Philadelphia? New York?
— Rex Sinquefield, Forbes, 2013[154]

Forget me, forget my face, forget my name.
— Bluebloods, 2017

[154] Rex Sinquefield, "The Earnings Tax is a Key Factor in Detroit's taxpayer Exodus, Bankruptcy," Forbes, August 11, 2013. https://www.forbes.com/sites/rexsinquefield/2013/08/11/the-earnings-tax-is-a-key-factor-in-detroits-taxpayer-exodus-bankruptcy/#3be175e04ae5

Section XI – California vs. Texas: A Tale of Two States

California: Oh What a Change
Net Migration Between California and Other States, 1955-1960 (red) and 1995-2000 (blue)

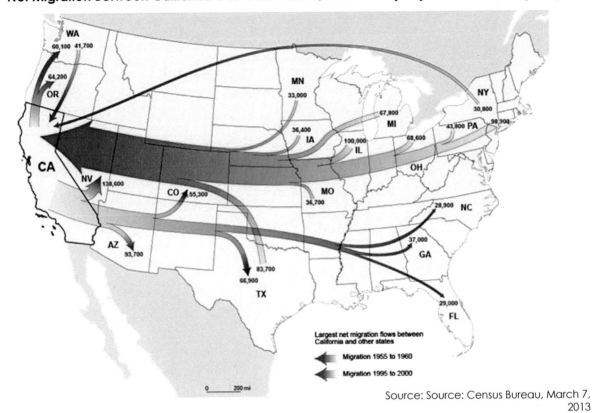

Largest net migration flows between California and other states

Migration 1955 to 1960

Migration 1995 to 2000

0   200 mi

Source: Source: Census Bureau, March 7, 2013

Taxes (2016)

	Highest %			Tax Progressivity	Dollars Per $1,000 of Personal Income			Dollars Per $100 of Payroll	
	PIT	Capital Gains	CIT	1: Best - 50: Worst	Property	Sales	Other	Avg. Workers' Comp.	Gift and Estate
California	13.3	13.3	8.8	50th	28.6	24.2	18.2	3.5	No
Texas	0	0	2.5	1st	35.9	24.2	20.6	1.6	No

Source: American Legislative Exchange Council, *Rich States, Poor States*, 9th Edition

Other Government Variables (2016)

	Right to Work	Spending % of GSP	Min. Wage	Public Emp. Per 10,000 Pop.	Fracking Permitted
California	No	20.9	10.00	452	No
Texas	Yes	14.7	7.25	533	Yes

Source: American Legislative Exchange Council, *Rich States, Poor States*, 9th Edition

Both California and Texas have huge oil reserves, yet California inhibits their development and Texas encourages it. As a result, the growth in oil production in Texas in recent years has been enormous. In California, oil production is still falling due to onerous regulations and restrictions.

That'll Teach You...Not!

They have learned the lesson of Proposition 13, which is that tax cuts are a prerequisite for cuts in government spending. The politics of the budgetary process is such that a cut in any particular program will provoke intense opposition from a minority, and only indifference from the majority. In such a case, it is unreasonable to expect politicians to pay the high political costs involved. They can only cut when they are seen to have no alternative.[155]
— Irving Kristol, 1978

California vs. Texas
(annual, 2014, "pay" is per full-time equivalent employee and "get" is number of full-time equivalent employees per 10,000 population)

CALIFORNIA	PAYS:	GETS:
Educators	40% More	31% Less
Police	59% More	3% Less
Hospital	50% More	Equal
Fire	67% More	14% Less
Highway	83% More	12% Less
Public Welfare	51% More	93% More
THAN TEXAS		

Source: Source: Census Bureau

	California	Texas
Standard Test Scores[156]	46th	32nd
Annual Cost of Prisoner[157]	$47,421	$21,390
Cost of 1 Mile of Highway[158]	$419,090	$177,357
Road Condition[159]	42nd	19th
Population on Welfare[160]	4.1%	1.8%
Poverty[161]	23.5%	16.5%

Source: Bureau of Labor Statistics, Census Bureau, Reason Foundation, Vera Institute of Justice

---

[155] Bruce Bartlett, "Supply-Side Economics: 'Voodoo Economics' or Lasting Contribution?" Laffer Associates, November 11, 2003.

[156] Data are for 2015, see: National Center for Education Statistics, "National Assessment of Educational Progress," 2015.

[157] Data are for 2010, see: Christian Henrichson and Ruth Delaney, "The Price of Prisons: What Incarceration Costs Taxpayers," Figure 4: The Taxpayer Costs of State Prisons per Inmate, Vera Institute of Justice, January 2012.

[158] Data are for 2013, see: David T. Hartgen, M. Gregory Fields and Baruch Feigenbaum, "22nd Annual Report on the Performance of State Highway Systems," Table 10: Total Disbursements per State-Controlled Mile, Reason Foundation, September 2016.

[159] Ibid, Table 3: 22nd Annual Highway Performance and Cost-Effectiveness Rankings

[160] Data arc for 2012, see: Shelley K. Irving, "Public Assistance Receipt 2000 to 2012," Table 1, U.S. Census Bureau, September 2014.

[161] Data are three-year average 2009-2011, U.S. Census Bureau, see: Arthur B. Laffer et al., "Fiscal Parasitic Leakages" in An Inquiry into the Nature and Causes of the Wealth of States, pg. 207, 2014.

Doesn't This Just Say It All?
United Van Lines Shipment Data

United Van Lines keeps close track of where its customers are moving and shipping their belongings to and from in terms of inbound and <u>outbound</u> moves for each state. In the chart below, states shaded red are those states where outbound shipments accounted for 55% or more of all shipments in 2005 and states shaded green are those states where <u>inbound</u> shipments accounted for 55% or more of all shipments in 2005. Doesn't this just say it all?

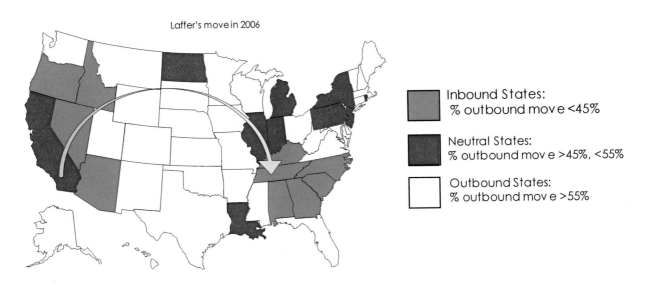

Laffer's move in 2006

Inbound States:
% outbound move <45%

Neutral States:
% outbound move >45%, <55%

Outbound States:
% outbound move >55%

After California Governor Arnold Schwarzenegger's "Capitulation to Socialism" State of the State address in January of 2006, Arthur Laffer made one of the most important decisions of his life: To leave California, to take his business and his extended family with him. Then came the hard part: just how does one really move a lifetime of accumulation from San Diego, CA to Nashville, TN? Being a control freak and having collected fossils, antiques and other perishable treasures, he was not about to hire professional movers. Never!

Around mid-year 2006 on the U-Haul website, the cost of renting a 26' moving van from San Diego, CA to Nashville, TN one way was over $2½ thousand, while renting the same truck from Nashville, TN to San Diego, CA was far less than one thousand dollars. But even more to the point, renting a 26' truck for 10 days with unlimited miles in California was around $2,000, yet in Tennessee, it was around $250.

Laffer (it was preferable to use Penske trucks, but the numbers were the same) rented trucks in

Nashville and had his employees speed across the country empty to San Diego. Once in San Diego, home and office furnishings were packed and the trucks were sent back to Nashville. Once in Nashville, the belongings were unloaded and the trucks returned to Penske. The savings were HUGE.

On one such occasion on returning his Penske truck, the incomparable Michael Madzin, in a suit and tie, was asked how many miles were on the odometer, to which Mr. Madzin retorted, "There are no mileage charges," and the rental agent agreed but indicated that he still needed the miles for the Penske files. Hearing the number of miles, the Penske representative shouted in disbelief "5000 miles?!" and Mr. Madzin in a soft voice replied, "I took side roads." The lesson: incentives matter.

Laffer and his family leaving California

Proposition 13—People Know Best!

California vs. U.S.: Excess State & Local Tax Burden vs. Excess Unemployment
California General Obligation Credit Rating

(annual, 1970 to 1988, excess tax burden is CA total taxes paid per $1,000 of personal income in excess of U.S. total taxes paid per $1,000 of personal income, excess unemployment is CA unemployment rate in excess of U.S. unemployment rate)

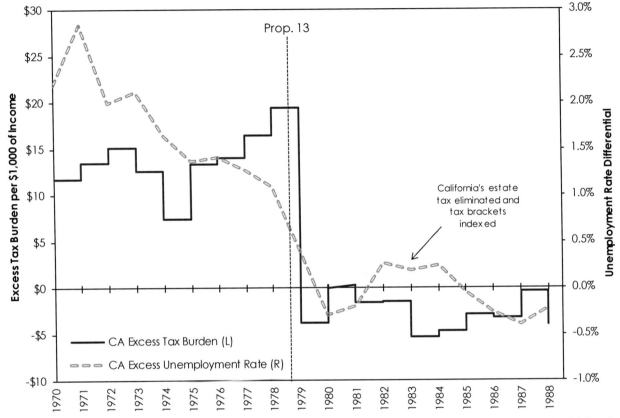

Source: California State Treasurer Public Finance Division, Census Bureau, Haver Analytics, Standard & Poor's

On June 8, 1978, California passed Proposition 13, which reduced property tax rates by close to 60% (from an average rate of 2.5% of market value to 1%). Harvard's fabled socialist Professor John Kenneth Galbraith sent Dr. Laffer a note with a gift of a toy fire engine, which he sarcastically said was intended to replace the real fire engines Proposition 13 would deprive the people of California. Little did he know what he portrayed as the coming Armageddon was, in fact, the Renaissance of the Golden State. Just look at the chart above and you'll see what we mean. And then, of course, there's always Walter Heller.

Chaotic cuts in local school, hospital, police and fire services would be the order of the day.

By putting legislators in such fiscal irons, the new constitutional tax limit would enfeeble government and weaken democracy....the effects of Jarvis-Gann would range from capricious to deplorable.

The UCLA econometric model also shows a loss of 300,000 local jobs, plus 100,000 private jobs, under Proposition 13.[162]
—*Walter Heller on Proposition 13*

The judgement of most moderate and responsible politicians is that the voters of California behaved in an immoderate and irresponsible manner by turning out in record numbers to pass Proposition 13...by a window-rattling 65% to 35% majority.[163]
—*Bill Schneider on Proposition 13*

[162] Walter Heller, "'Meat-Axe Radicalism' in California," in The Economics of the Tax Revolt, ed. Arthur B. Laffer & Jan P. Seymour, p. 124, 1979.
[163] William Schneider, "Punching Through the Jarvis Myth," in The Economics of the Tax Revolt, ed. Arthur B. Laffer & Jan P. Seymour, p. 114, 1979.

Detroit

The below photos are quite humorously captioned: *"It's easier to come back from a nuclear strike than five decades of Democrat control of government."*[164] However, the state of dispair and destruction that result from either nuclear weapons or anti-growth policies should be taken as anything BUT a laughing matter. The below images are not funny but they do tell a story.

1945

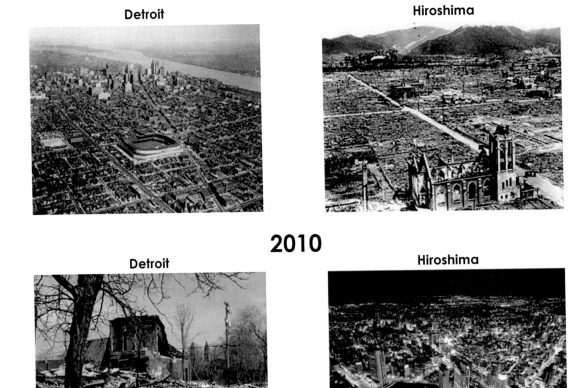

Per Aeschylus in his play Agamemnon:

*And even in our sleep, pain that cannot forget
falls drop by drop upon the heart,
and in our own despair, against our will,
comes wisdom to us by the awful grace of God.*[165]

Supply-side economics is meant to unleash the prosperity and growth that people so desperately deserve, yet government continues to obstruct. In destroying the competitiveness of countries, states, or cities, anti-growth policies are also destroying lives. Let Detroit serve as an example of what we should strive as hard as possible NOT to do.

---

[164] "Yesterday Was The 67th Anniversary of the Hiroshima Bomb," The Hayride, August 7, 2012. http://thehayride.com/2012/08/yesterday-was-the-67th-anniversary-of-the-hiroshima-bomb/
[165] Translated by Edith Hamilton, "The Greek Way, "The Greek Way of Writing," pg. 61, 1930.

44786071R00093

Made in the USA
San Bernardino, CA
22 July 2019